Noah
Study Guide

Flying Eagle Publications

Flying **Eagle**
Publications
flyingeaglepublications.com

Noah Study Guide
Print ISBN: 978-1-7327-688-8-8

Table of Contents

Introduction to Study Guide

We like choices. In this guide we've given you the ability to adapt it to your purpose. Do you need discussion questions for a youth or small group study? Or a more formalized way of assessing learning because you are a homeschool or private school educator? Perhaps you are interested in pursuing your own spiritual growth? Will you need ideas for further study?

We've got you covered.

While any of the questions may be used to enhance discussions of the reading material, most are geared toward academic learning for the purpose of apologetics. Tests are provided if you need them. Answers to most questions are at the back of the book. Obviously some questions are meant for personal reflection and the answers to these will vary.

The Devotion and Drawing Near Sections are provided to enhance learning and to help students relate the subject matter to themselves. They are to be completed at the same time.

The For Further Study and Activity sections are optional. One or two could be chosen and assigned as part of the overall course or as weekly group projects for small groups, co-ops or classrooms. A lesson plan for homeschooling is provided as an example for a weekly course with tests to evaluate learning. This plan could be adapted for the classroom.

Of course no adult in a small group or otherwise wants to have to do formal projects and tests, so ignore all the heavy duty school lingo. Gather the discussion material you want to use for each session, use an activity to break up the weekly routine if you wish, and choose an application so people can interact with Jesus. We've provided a lesson template for you to organize your thoughts. Happy learning!

Leader Guide

We've created two pathways to use this guide in an academic or home-school setting. They are listed below. A daily assignment schedule follows. We recommend Guided Learning for the best results. You can, however, adapt and blend either method to create an individualized experience.

Guided Learning: *Pre-assign reading of full chapter on student's time. Do not follow reading schedule.* This method allows for the student to read the chapter as a whole. After they've completed the chapter, discuss portions of the chapter each day as the Assignment Schedule instructs to reinforce learning. Student may read the Devotion from the Study Guide on first day of each chapter discussion. Use the daily schedule to review information contained in the chapter and to discuss assigned questions. Talk about any points, facts or discoveries you or the student(s) think are important for that portion. Assign an Activity or Further Study as a project for the week. This may be a group project if desired. Use the Chapter Evaluation to record or assess learning. Test may be used as a quiz on Day 4 and corrected. Reteach any problem areas. Take test again on Day 5.

- Teacher Responsibility: Be familiar with material. Make sure chapter gets read before daily discussion schedule starts. Guide daily discussions 20-30 minutes. Assign any Activities or Further Studies for week and discuss or check. Reteach any problem areas. Conduct whichever testing procedure you prefer. *Bonus Teacher Tip:* Use answer key section when asking students questions because the answer is right in front of you– just in case you forgot the material. This saves time and boy, do you look smart!

- Student Responsibility: Read book and Devotion from Study Guide. Take notes of any information desired. Partake in discussion. Give presentation of completed Activity or Further Study. Keep a folder for all material. Complete review and evaluation for chapter.

Independent Student Learning: Have student keep a notebook to answer the assigned questions. Use the daily schedule to assign reading and questions. Check each day's questions. Choose Activity or Further Study to be completed for each chapter. These are optional, if pressed for time. They may also be completed on student's own time and shared or collected when you choose. Student should take test after chapter work is completed.

- Teacher's Responsibility: Prepare for successful learning. Photocopy assignment schedule, questions and test for student if they are not using the Study Guide. Check answers to daily questions so student is reviewing correct information. Assign Activity or Further Study for the week and check. Check test answers.

- Student's Responsibility: Keep a folder of all material. Complete daily readings, assigned questions, activity projects and review. Review and take test after each chapter.

Assignment Schedule

- Read pages listed to quotation that marks the last paragraph to be read for the day. Continue from next paragraph on following day. On Day 4 you will finish reading the chapter.
- Complete questions assigned for each day after reading selection.
- Guided Learning students should read Devotion from Study Guide on Day 1 for each chapter and be ready to discuss questions assigned for the page content covered for Days 1-4 for each chapter.

Chapter 1 What Noah Knew

Day 1: Read pgs 1-4 to "Man Could Write." Answer questions 1-7. Read Devotion in *Study Guide*.
Day 2: Read pgs 4-9 to "Man Betrayed God." Answer questions 8-18.
Day 3: Read pgs 9-12 to "The Result of Man's Betrayal." Answer questions 19-24.
Day 4: Read pgs 12-15. Answer questions 25-35.
Day 5: Review and take test.

Chapter 2 Noah's World

Day 1: Read pgs 17-19 to "But the land Noah lived on did not look like our world." Answer questions 1-4. Read Devotion in *Study Guide*.
Day 2: Read pgs 19-22 to "But there is no need to place him in Africa first." Answer questions 5-13.

Day 3: Read pgs 22-25 to "Murder was common." Answer questions 17-27.

Day 4: Read pgs 26-28. Answer questions 28-30.

Day 5: Review and take test.

Chapter 3 Preacher of Righteousness

Day 1: Read pgs 29-32 to "He gave God first place in his life." Answer questions 1-4. Read Devotion in *Study Guide*.

Day 2: Read pgs 33-36 to "What is your guess?" Answer questions 5-13.

Day 3: Read pgs 37-40 to "...they would have been lost." Answer questions 14-26.

Day 4: Read pgs 41-43. Answer questions 27-35.

Day 5: Review and take test.

Chapter 4 After The Flood

Day 1: Read pgs 45-48 to "...ranging from 70% to 30%." Answer questions 1-13. Read Devotion in *Study Guide*.

Day 2: Read pgs 48-52 to "...problem solvers in their new world." Answer questions 14-22.

Day 3: Read pgs 52-56 to "...means the tower of confusion." Answer questions 23-33.

Day 4: Read pgs 56-59. Answer questions 34-40.

Day 5: Review and take test(s).

Chapter 5 Flood Stories

Day 1: Read pgs 61-64 to "...a hero based on a real person or group." Answer questions 1-6. Read Devotion in *Study Guide*.

Day 2: Read pgs 64-68 to " He wrote the story on stone tablets." Answer questions 7-15.

Day 3: Read pgs 68-73 to "...separated by thousands and millions of years." Answer questions 16-22.

Day 4: Read pgs 73-75. Answer questions 23-30.

Day 5: Review and take test.

Chapter 6 City Builders

Day 1: Read pgs 77-80. Answer questions 1-7. Read Devotion in *Study Guide*.

Day 2: Read pgs 81-84 to "...when they traveled west." Answer questions 8-18.

Day 3: Read pgs 84-88. Answer questions 19-29.

Day 4: Read pgs 89-91. Answer question 30.

Day 5: Review and take test.

Chapter 7 Empire Builders

Day 1: Read pgs 93-97 to "...Babylonian Captivity in 605BC." Answer questions 1-9. Read Devotion in *Study Guide.*

Day 2: Read pgs 97-101 to "...the location may be significant." Answer questions 10-17.

Day 3: Read pgs 101-105 to "...never ending creativity of evolution." Answer questions 18-26.

Day 4: Read pgs 105-111. Answer questions 27-30.

Day 5: Review and take test. Time to celebrate! You are done!

Group Leader Template

To Do: Read chapter from book and Devotion from Study Guide. Pray for students and for wisdom.

To List: Chapter and Devotion high points, facts, discoveries I thought important and note the page number of each. These are my talking points, but I will ask my students what they learned from the chapter too and include their input throughout the lesson.

To Choose: The verses I am focusing on and will teach from.

To Decide: What I want the class to know and remember. This is my teaching focus. Will I use the Drawing Near application?

To Pick: Questions I want to cover and discuss. (Tip: Have the *Guide* with you in case you have time to ask more than you have chosen.)

To Pick: At least one activity to do during discussion time to provide variety to class flow. I can break up class into groups for this. (Tip: Always plan more than you think you will need in case you have to fill time.)

To Remember: Some students will not have read the portion for the week or I may have new students, so I am ready to explain, explain and patiently explain.

My Notes:

Chapter 1

What Noah Knew

Devotion

Have your Bible, a journal and pen handy. Look up the verses quoted. Read them, the verses around them, and write down what you learn.

It is said that knowledge is power, and that is right most of the time. The problem is the quality of the power depends on the quality of the knowledge.

In parts of the western United States a person can be described as being all hat and no cattle. This means the person looks like he should know what needs to be done, but he has no substance, no power to deliver or no deeds to back up what he appears to be. This is a person with the wrong kind of knowledge.

The power knowledge wields can be influence, a way to get wealth or a way to fulfill a need. Power can be used for good, or it can be used selfishly.

Action: Can you think of examples?

When you possess the right knowledge, it will be true and will not change with the circumstances. Sometimes this is referred to as a principle or truth. But we must be careful not to confuse truth with facts. Facts can be true and still change. For example, John is hungry. John is hungry is a fact. John eats his lunch and then the fact "John is hungry" is no longer true.

The people of Noah's day had knowledge. They were not ignorant men and women who could only grunt, point and smack their dinner over the head with a club or pluck it from a tree with grimy hands. They expressed their thoughts in a complex language and shared their knowledge with others. But the Bible tells us most of them were loyal to the wrong kind of knowledge, and it gave them the wrong kind of power.

These people knew their world; how it worked to a certain degree so they could plant, grow, build and create. They were familiar with what they could see, touch and experience. They based their life on these facts. They based what they believed to be truth on these things.

And they did have power. Kings ruled. Cities were built. People increased what they owned. Families multiplied. But their knowledge didn't save them. Their power had no might in the end. They were all hat and no cattle.

Noah had a different knowledge with a different power. His knowledge wasn't based on what he could see, feel, touch or experience. It was based on what God told him. This is called revelation knowledge because it was given to him. It was revealed.

Noah was loyal to the knowledge God gave him and by it, he was loyal to the One who had given him the words. This revelation knowledge saved Noah and his family. It kept them safe through a world-wide disaster. Noah chose the knowledge he believed, and it saved his life.

Perhaps a better way to describe the relationship between knowledge and power is the knowledge you choose is the power you will know.

The people stranded outside the ark had one hundred years to hear Noah's story and choose what they believed about it. There were probably some people that kind of believed it, but they did not act on their belief. They never joined in with Noah. Maybe as the floods began, they pointed an accusing finger at God and blamed him for their predicament. But they never chose His words or power to save them.

We are fortunate to have God's words to us written down so we can read them whenever we want. We can read John 14:6. " 'I am the way, the truth, and the life!' Jesus answered. 'Without me, no one can go to the Father.' " (CEV) We can ponder Colossians 1:17. "God's Son was before all else, and by him everything is held together." (CEV)

We have the revelation knowledge of the Bible sold in bookstores, available free online, on shelves in libraries and offered free from ministries. We can listen to it on various devices in a variety of ways. But the question is do you value it?

Wisdom is the ability to know what to do with knowledge. Discernment is being able to distinguish or judge between things. You cannot have either without truth.

When you read the Bible your mind is being taught truth. Jesus is Truth and He is the Living Word. Romans 12:2 advises us, "...be not conformed to this world: but be ye transformed by the renewing of your mind, that ye may prove what is that good, and acceptable, and perfect, will of God."

God's word is powerful to the degree you value it. The people banging on the ark in the pouring rain heard God's words, considered them. But they did not value them enough to act on them.

Drawing Near Activity: Ask yourself, "What place do I give God's word? Is it first— a spacious place where I read it and allow it to teach me? Do I desire to value God's word and the knowledge He wants to give me?" Turn your answers into a prayer to God.

Remember, when you open the Bible to read God's word, you are in the presence of God. God says in Psalm 138:2 He magnifies His word above His name. His word is alive with power to teach you and to give you a spirit of wisdom and revelation because it was written by Holy Spirit, the possessor of wisdom and revelation. (2Timothy 3:16 and Proverbs 8)

As you read the Bible, ask Holy Spirit to show you God's knowledge and its power to save.

Chapter 1 General Questions

1. Who collected the histories and wrote them down in the book of Genesis?

2. When did man begin speaking a language?

3. What is a complex language?

4. What was evolutionists' theory about languages?

5. What is the language principle?

6. How old are languages and what is a Christian's reason for this approximate date?

7. How many languages did people living directly after the flood speak?

Activity: Find a short sentence from your favorite book. Using crayons or markers and paper, create your own pictograph to write this sentence. Do not use known letters or words. You are creating your own language using symbols to tell the meaning of the sentence. Notice what skills you need to do this. Share your sentence with your family or a friend.

8. What is the oldest known alphabet?

9. Describe the discovery at Serabit el-Khadim?

10. What is the Bible's Hebrew storytelling method?

11. Is this method found outside the Bible? If yes, where?

Activity: You can view the modern Hebrew alphabet on the *Jewish Virtual Library* website. Type "Hebrew" or "Hebrew Alphabet" into their search bar. The Hebrew *alef-bet* has no vowels. The language is written right to left. That is opposite of English. Each Hebrew letter is also a number, a picture and a word. It certainly is an ancient language, and it is complex. Try copying the Hebrew *alef-bet* from a chart. Remember, start on the right and move left.

12. What is the meaning of *towlĕdah* and how is the word used in the Bible?

13. Why are the Nuzi Tablets important to the family histories recorded in Genesis?

For Further Study:

Nuzi was once part of the Mitanni Empire. Today it is called Yorghan Tepe, and it is located in northern Iraq in a region known as Iraqi Kurdistan. Kurdistan is a region including northern Iraq, northern Syria, southeast Turkey and northwest Iran. The majority of people living in these regions call themselves Kurds. Their territory has always been near the Zagros and Taurus Mountains.

Erbil (er BEEL) is a city you may have heard of in the news. It is in Iraq. Did you know it is the capital of Iraqi Kurdistan and the home of the Kurds' governing body, the Kurdish Regional Government? Erbil is said to be one of the oldest continuously inhabited cities on the earth.[1]

It may seem odd that the Kurds decided to have their own government when they were already living in other countries with governments like Iraq, Syria, Turkey and Iran. But they have shared their region with many ancient people like the Guti and Armenians and hung on to their culture all this time. Today they are still struggling to keep it.

---

[1] "Erbil." The Kurdish Project. https://thekurdishproject.org/kurdistan-map/iraqi-kurdistan/erbil/

See if you can locate a map showing the region of Kurdistan. Can you find Yorghan Tepe? You might like to try some Kurdish food. While goat's head may not sound good, maybe you would like to make some rice and wrap it in grape leaves or eat flatbread and drink tea with honey. Or, you could make a tomato and yogurt sauce for your next chicken dinner.[2]

14. How long did people live in the era before the flood and after?

Activity: Read Genesis 9:29 and Genesis 11:10-32. Make a chart of the men's names and ages. What is the youngest recorded age of death before the flood? How long did Noah live? When did men begin to live shorter lives?

15. Why is man not equal to animals?

---

[2] "Kurdish Food." The Kurdish Project. https://thekurdishproject.org/history-and-culture/kurdish-culture/kurdish-food/

For Further Study:

Read Psalm 8. In Psalm 8:5 the word translated angels in most Bibles are the Hebrew *min* (part of; from; out of) and *'ĕlôhîym* (a word used for the Supreme God). Green's *Literal Translation of the Bible* reads, "For You have made him lack a little from God; and have crowned him with glory and honor." Now read the chapter again. How does this change your understanding of the Psalm? What does this verse mean to you?

16. How might the story of creation been recorded?

17. Does the Bible support an old earth?

18. Describe the Garden of Eden. Where might it be?

19. Does the Bible tell us about all of Adam's sons?

20. Who was Cain and what was he like?

21. Who was Lucifer and what was his plan?

22. What didn't Adam and Eve know about?

23. Was Adam deceived?

24. What didn't Adam realize before he decided to disobey God?

25. Why did Adam and Eve have to leave the Garden?

26. When Cain sinned and killed Abel how might it have reminded Adam of his sin?

27. Why did God want the creation account and Adam's history written down?

28. What else did God give man when He created him that gives man the ability to choose?

29. How does sin influence our world?

30. What are the two deaths Adam and Eve experienced?

31. What was God's promise to Adam and Eve after they had sinned?

32. How many years passed before this promise was fulfilled?

33. Who was the Deliverer?

34. List the things Noah knew.

35. What is the gift called that God provided through His Deliverer?

Chapter Evaluation

Student may write what they learned from this chapter, using a paragraph essay format. Suggested: 500 words or one page. Alternative: Student may give an oral report or Charlotte Mason style narration. Or student may complete the test provided below.

Chapter 1 Test

1. When did man begin speaking a language?

2. What is evolutionists' theory about languages?

3. What is the language principle?

4. How old are languages and what is a Christian's reason for this approximate date?

5. What is the oldest known alphabet?

6. What is the Bible's Hebrew storytelling method?

7. What is the meaning of *towlĕdah* and how is the word used in the Bible?

8. Why are the Nuzi Tablets important to the family histories recorded in Genesis?

9. What are the two deaths Adam and Eve experienced?

10. List the things Noah knew.

• Chapter 2 •

Noah's World

Devotion

Have your Bible, a journal and pen handy. Look up the verses quoted. Read them, the verses around them, and write down what you learn.

When you think of evil, you probably imagine the worst, scariest things. But sometimes evil can look average, ordinary, even like day to day life.

We can think of it as evil is what wickedness produces. Wicked in English is related to the word witch and the Old English wicca or wizard. Evil is not limited to wicked witches and wizards, of course. Noah Webster's *1828 American Dictionary Of The English Language* tells us wicked is indeed the Saxon wican which means to stumble, to depart, to fall away. It is to wind and turn; to waver (vacillate).

Stumbling, falling away and wavering was most likely not what you imagined when you heard the word evil, right? To God —and not just the Saxons— this is what wickedness is. Proverbs 6:12-19 is a good summary of everything displeasing to God, and it gives us a picture of a wicked man. "A naughty person, a wicked man, walketh with a froward mouth. He winketh with his eyes, he speaketh with his feet, he teacheth with his fingers; Frowardness is in his heart, he deviseth mischief continually; he soweth discord." (Proverbs 6:12-14)

Let's take a look at what some of these words mean in Hebrew, the language of the Old Testament. And just in case you've never heard of the word froward, it describes a person who makes disobedience and opposition their habit. Naughty is *b^elîya'al* (bah LEE yah ell), without profit, ungodly. Wicked is *'âven* (ahVEHN), to pant, to exert oneself in vain, trouble, vanity, evil, wickedness, mischief. Froward is *'iqq^eshûth* (Ick aySHOOTH), perverse (from *'iqqēš*, twisted, distorted). Frowardness is *tahpûkâh* (tap ew KHAW), perversity, fraud (from *hâphak*, to turn). Mischief is ra' (ra or rah) and *râ'âh* (rah AH), bad, evil, displeasing, harm, sad, mischief, trouble, wrong, wicked.

The Hebrew shows us the same idea of wickedness as being to turn, and twisted. Notice that this evil can be wrong, distorted and displeasing. It doesn't have to be on the level of committing murder.

But it is ungodly and without profit. It can be wavering which is like losing determination, purpose or being unable to decide between two opinions. The Bible describes wavering as doubt, something Jesus warned people not to do. This is the type of wickedness that is subtle.

The teacher who teaches evolution in opposition to God does not look evil. They seem ordinary. They are average people like the ones we meet everyday. The person who doubts God is said to be honest. He is praised for admitting his feelings, and so he writes a best selling book accusing God of crimes against mankind. The person who believes a woman should have the right to abort a baby may be a parent themselves. Average. Ordinary.

Action: Take a minute and think of the everyday distortions of truth we are familiar with.

Here is Proverbs 6:12-14 in the *International Standard Bible*: "A worthless man, a wicked man, goes around with devious speech, winking with his eyes, making signs with his feet, pointing with his fingers, planning evil with a perverse mind, continually stirring up discord." (ISV)

This worthless wicked person deceives others with his mouth. He has set himself against God. He may not know it. He may be convinced he is right and contributing to society. But God sees him as a worthless fraud spreading lies. This type of pride is something God hates. He hates it because it harms people, the people peddling it included.

"Here are six things that the LORD hates—seven, in fact, are detestable to him: Arrogant eyes, a lying tongue and hands shedding innocent blood; a heart crafting evil plans, feet running swiftly to wickedness, a false witness snorting lies, and someone sowing quarrels between brothers." (Proverbs 6:16-19 ISV)

Let's study this a bit further. Hate is *śānē'* (sahnAY) which means hate, enemy, foe. God considers these foes disgusting (*tō'ēbah* toe ay VAH). Pride, lying, hands that shed innocent blood, a heart (will, intellect) that devises wicked (*'āven*) designs/purposes, feet that run to do evil mischief (*rā'āh*), a person who lies about another person to their harm, and someone who creates strife among people.

In Noah's day wicked people were the majority. They had turned from God in pride and twisted the truth. It resulted in evil mischief that produced harm and trouble. The person who chose to be opposed to God became His enemy. In doing so, they decided their future.

"Therefore, disaster will overtake him suddenly. He will be broken in an instant, and he will never recover." (Proverbs 6:15)

The important thing about the subtle kind of wickedness is it opens the door to real evil. Beliefs create thoughts. Thoughts lead to actions. God says He sees the end from the beginning, so to God the thought is the action. (Matthew 5:21-28) This is why we need to guard the ideas we accept. Colossians 2:8 states, "Take care lest there be some one who leads you away as prisoners by means of his philosophy and idle fancies, following human traditions and the world's crude notions instead of following Christ." (WNT)

A prisoner is in bondage. We are not to be bound, made slaves to lies taught by worthless wicked people opposed to God. You can pray for them. Just don't agree with them.

The people who lived before the flood were the average people of their day doing average things. They did it in the midst of the violence and the lies. Jesus said, "For as in the days that were before the flood they were eating and drinking, marrying and giving in marriage, until the day that [Noah] entered into the ark, And knew not until the flood came, and took them all away; so shall also the coming of the Son of man be." (Matthew 24:38-39)

Jesus tells us it will be the same way near to the time He comes again. This is why knowing about Noah and the flood is important to you. We do not know the exact time Jesus is coming just like Noah did not know the exact day the rain would begin. But he knew rain was coming, and he was prepared.

Action: Right now, put yourself under the magnifying glass and ask yourself some important questions.

Am I being deceived by lies that are taught to me by men opposed to God?

Do my thoughts agree with God's ways?

Does my behavior reflect what God values?

Do I know what God values?

Drawing Near Activity: Write down your honest answers to these questions. Ask God to help you live for Him. He has provided for your victory if you trust Him and lean on Him everyday. When King David was just a young boy taking care of sheep he loved the Lord. He prayed a prayer you can pray yourself. He prayed, "Let my words and my thoughts be pleasing to you, LORD, because you are my mighty rock and my protector." (Psalm 19:14 CEV)

Chapter 2 General Questions

1. What is the Gap Theory of creation?

2. What is the age of time the Bible tells us about?

3. When did James Ussher and others think the earth was created?

4. What did Cain do after he had to leave the area where Adam and Eve were living?

5. What did Antonio Snider-Pellegrini discover?

6. What is a Super Continent?

7. Is Snider-Pellegrini's theory accepted?

8. What is the name of Snider-Pellegrini's map?

9. How do geologists know where the continents fit together?

10. What is the name given to the map geologists agree on?

11. Are these maps perfectly reliable?

Activity: Trace a map of the world and cut apart the seven continents. Can you fit them together? Look at the illustrations of Pangaea and Rodinia in the book, *NOAH*. How well did you do? If you like, research what scientist think about the supercontinent cycle.

12. Describe what the Super Continent was like.

13. What does fossilized tree resin tell us about the earth's temperature?

14. What creatures did Noah take with him on the ark?

15. How many people do we estimate were on the earth in Noah's time?

16. What did ancient people look like?

17. Who is Cheddar Man?

18. What are theories about Cheddar Man and why does scientist Mark Thomas disagree?

For Further Study:

According to *Smithsonian Magazine*, Cheddar Man is the oldest complete skeleton discovered in England.[1] The facial reconstruction of his image portrays him as a pleasant sort of guy. Even handsome in a rugged way. The important thing to notice is he looks like someone who could walk down a street in London today. But that is not what the scientists think, the scientists Mark Thomas disagrees with.

Research Cheddar Man and find a picture of him. What do you think? Is he so different than someone you might meet today?

19. Where do evolutionists think man began to live on the earth?

20. What archaeological evidence upsets their theory?

---

[1] Brigit Katz. "Early Briton Had Dark Skin and Light Eyes, DNA Analysis Shows." *Smithsonian Magazine*. February 7. 2018. https://www.smithsonianmag.com/smart-news/ancient-briton-had-dark-skin-and-light-eyes-dna-analysis-shows-180968097/

21. What can we be sure of about ancient man?

22. Who was Lamech and what was he like?

23. What changed when Adam changed masters?

24. Who was Enosh and what did people begin doing during his lifetime?

25. Describe the giants living in the pre-flood world and those living after.

26. What began to happen to the people living before the flood? (Genesis 6:5)

27. Who was Sanchuniathon and what was the world like that he wrote about?

For Further Study:

    Once there was a mysterious city. Archaeologists read about it on cylinders and engraved tablets. The ancient texts of Mari and Ebla told its glories. A gate with large columns greeted the visitor from the west as he entered the city. He could gaze up at two story houses lining the streets.[2] He might stop at the temples dedicated to the pagan gods Baal and Dagon. But the palace would capture his attention above all else. Its large pillared hall, its beautifully crafted stone walls and courtyards impressed even kings.[3]

Foreign merchants from Cyprus and Crete made this city their home. Kings and traders spoke of it in their ledgers. Trade was very big business in this city. But there was a problem. None of the archaeologists or historians knew where this city was. They didn't know where to look, where to start digging. It was thought of as a lost city, the lost city of Ugarit.

Then one day a farmer in Syria began plowing a field when his plow hit a rock. All good farmers clear rocks from their field. But as he bent down to unearth the rock, he realized it was not a rock. It was a brick, and there was a gaping hole beneath it. He had uncovered an ancient tomb. Inside were treasures like he had only dreamed of. Gold, silver, ivory, ornate jugs and vases. He was rich or so he had hoped, because when he tried to sell his valuables, the police reported it to French archaeologists.[4]

And, just like that, a lost city wasn't lost any more. The farmer had found Ugarit.

---

[2] Department of Ancient Near Eastern Art. "Ugarit." In *Heilbrunn Timeline of Art History*. New York: The Metropolitan Museum of Art, 2000–. http://www.metmuseum.org/toah/hd/ugar/hd_ugar.htm (October 2004)

[3] Marguerite Yon. "Ugarit: 6,000 Years of History." *Near Eastern Archaeology* 63, no. 4 (2000): 187–89. https://doi.org/10.2307/3210775.

[4] Justin King. "Ugarit." *World History Encyclopedia*. Last modified March 22, 2012. https://www.worldhistory.org/ugarit/.

The French archaeologists may have been disappointed at first. The tomb the farmer discovered had nothing much to offer. But they kept digging. Then they heard a local legend about a mound. Five days of excavation later, the first of Ugarit's tablets were discovered.[5]

What has been discovered at Ugarit is important to Bible scholars because it has revealed the Canaanite culture just as the Old Testament described it, and all because a plow hit a stone— er, brick.

28. In Noah's world people lived very long lives. Is there archaeological evidence for this?

29. What is the problem with the Sumerian King List and how might it be solved?

30. Briefly describe Noah's world.

---

[5] Justin King. "Ugarit."

Chapter Evaluation

Student may write what they learned from this chapter, using a paragraph essay format. Suggested: 500 words or one page. Alternative: Student may give an oral report or Charlotte Mason style narration. Or student may complete the test provided below.

Chapter 2 Test

1. When did James Ussher and others think the earth was created?

2. What did Antonio Snider-Pellegrini discover?

3. What is a Super Continent?

4. How do geologists know where the continents fit together and are their maps perfectly reliable?

5. What does fossilized tree resin tell us about the earth's temperature?

6. Who is Cheddar Man?

7. What are theories about Cheddar Man and why does scientist Mark Thomas disagree?

8. Where do evolutionists think man began to live on the earth and what archaeological evidence upsets their theory?

9. Who was Sanchuniathon and what was the world like that he wrote about?

10. In Noah's world people lived very long lives. Is there archaeological evidence for this? If so, is there a problem with it and how might it be solved?

Chapter 3

Preacher of Righteousness

Devotion

Have your Bible, a journal and pen handy. Look up the verses quoted. Read them, the verses around them, and write down what you learn.

How do you preach righteousness while you build a ship no one thinks you need?

Good question. But first let's define righteousness.

Righteousness is innocence, holiness. It is being right and just. Mankind is not righteous on his own. He has to be made righteous, and this comes by grace through faith. "For by grace are ye saved through faith; and that not of yourselves: it is the gift of God." (Ephesians 2:8)

Righteousness is given to us when we believe what God says and we do what He told us to do. It is God's gift to us, and He declares us innocent. We sometimes call this innocence justification, and it describes the process of us being made right with God.

Noah preached righteousness by what he did: he believed what God said. Sounds simple, but it probably wasn't. Noah had to believe what he had never seen. He had to believe despite all of his neighbors and most of his family thinking he was crazy. And, he had to stand in this belief for a hundred years in the midst of pressure to conform to what everyone else believed.

When you hear something over and over by a large crowd, you can get used to it. You can become weary of resisting. You can lose strength in your inner man and compromising starts to look like the right thing to do.

But intense pressure requires increased resistance. To stay strong you must have nourishment. For the believer that means focusing on what God says above anything or anyone else. We "feed" on God's word.

We would say Noah had to walk by faith. Walking is something you do everyday. You move from one place to another. You do it step by step or bit by bit. Faith in the Bible is believing in and trusting what God has said despite what you see. It is believing God's word, alone.

Noah believed as he moved forward in his life everyday, bit by bit. He believed in the morning, at noon, in the night. He believed when times were good and when times were bad. He never let go of what he believed by speaking something else or accepting some other idea. He did this day after day.

So, we say this is walking by faith. This is what Enoch did too. He was taken by God to heaven without dying. Raptured is the word we use for this. If you are alive and walking in faith when Jesus calls believers to come to heaven, you will be raptured too. You will be kept safe in heaven while trouble comes to people still living on earth. Noah was saved from a flood and kept safe in the ark while trouble came to those on the earth.

God is merciful to all. He has made a way for anyone to receive His mercy and love if they believe what He says and put their trust in Jesus. When people do this they are made right because God gives them His righteousness. He is able to gift them with mercy and righteousness. He is not able if a person does not believe what He says.

Everyday Noah showed what righteousness was when he took up his tools to work on the ark. When he answered questions and spoke of the flood God told him about, he was an example of righteousness. His actions preached. His loyalty to God's word preached. His words testified to the belief he hung on to in his heart. No one could take it from him.

His response to God's mercy was a trust that never wavered and a hope that never grew dim. He wasn't embarrassed to devote his life to obedience to God's word, and he wasn't ashamed that he did. Paul the Apostle made obedience to God's word his goal too. He said, "For I am not ashamed of the gospel of Christ: for it is the power of God unto salvation to every one that believeth." (Romans 1:16) To that, Noah would say, "Amen."

And that's how you preach righteousness while you build a ship no one thinks you need.

Drawing Near Activity: Answer the questions below.
In what ways do you preach righteousness to those around you?

Have you ever been embarrassed to be a Christian? If yes, why?

How can you strengthen yourself to be loyal to God even if no one around you is?

Write a prayer to God including your concerns, ideas and desires about the questions above or anything you have learned in this devotion.

Chapter 3 General Questions

1. Why might Noah's father have given him a name that means rest? (Remember, Noah's father's name was Lamech. But he was not the same man as the Lamech who had two wives and was Cain's grandson.)

2. Who was Enoch and what happened to him?

3. What began happening to Noah's family, his sisters, brothers, cousins, nieces and nephews? What did Noah decide to do instead?

4. How does Genesis 6:9 describe Noah?

5. What does it mean that Noah was "perfect in his generations?"

6. How old was Noah when his first son was born?

7. What did God tell Noah to do?

8. What is a cubit?

Activity: Measure the length of your arm from your elbow to the tip of your fingers. How close are you to the average measurement? Measure someone else and compare theirs with yours. Are the measurements close? Using string, cardboard or sticks, build something using your cubit as the measure.

9. How big was the ship Noah built?

10. What does *têbâh* mean and how is it used in Noah's story?

11. Is there any evidence in history and archaeology of large ships similar to the size of the ark? If yes, describe one.

12. Could Noah have used metal in the building of the ark? Why or why not?

13. What substance did God tell Noah to use to coat the ark?

14. What is this substance and why was it used?

15. In Genesis 6:14-16, God says to pitch the ark inside and outside with pitch. But the first pitch is the Hebrew verb *kâphar*. What does *kâphar* mean?

16. Did Noah know why he was to build a huge ship called an ark?

17. How long did it take Noah and his sons to build the ark?

18. What is surprising about the place Noah built the ark?

19. What does it mean to walk by faith?

20. What does Genesis 6:22 say about Noah and why do you think it is important?

21. What does the Bible mean when it says Noah was a preacher of righteousness?

Activity: Pretend you are a news reporter. Write an article about Noah and his mission or prepare a "night-time news report" and give your presentation to others.

22. How old was Noah's father Lamech when he died and why might his age be significant?

23. Who was Methuselah and what does his name mean?

24. What is important about the year Methuselah died?

25. How many animals might have been on the ark?

26. Why is it important that the ark had only one door?

27. After Noah boarded the ark with his wife, his sons and their wives, how long was it until the flooding rains came?

28. Who shut the door of the ark?

29. What might those inside the ark have been thinking about as the rain began? How about those outside the ark?

30. Describe the rain as the Bible defines it.

31. How many years passed from the creation of Adam to the flood? What year might this be on our timeline called BC or Before Christ?

32. What promise did God give Noah after he left the ark?

33. According to Ezekiel 1:28 and Revelation 4:3, where else can this symbol of the promise be found?

34. How does God's promise in Isaiah 54:9 apply to us?

For further study:

Read Revelation 20. In Revelation 20 it talks about a day similar to the day when God shut the door of the ark. What is this day?

35. What should we do in response to God's love and mercy?

Chapter Evaluation

Student may write what they learned from this chapter, using a paragraph essay format. Suggested: 500 words or one page. Alternative: Student may give an oral report or Charlotte Mason style narration. Or student may complete the test provided below.

Chapter 3 Test

1. How does Genesis 6:9 describe Noah?

2. What does it mean that Noah was "perfect in his generations?"

3. What is a cubit?

4. Describe the rain as the Bible defines it.

5. How many years passed from the creation of Adam to the flood? What year might this be on our timeline called BC or Before Christ?

6. What promise did God give Noah after he left the ark? According to Ezekiel 1:28 and Revelation 4:3, where else can this symbol of the promise be found?

7. Is there any evidence in history and archaeology of large ships similar to the size of the ark? If yes, describe one.

8. Could Noah have used metal in the building of the ark? Why or why not?

9. What does Genesis 6:22 say about Noah and why do you think it is important?

10. In Genesis 6:14-16, God says to pitch the ark inside and outside with pitch. But the first pitch is the Hebrew verb *kaphar.* What does *kaphar* mean?

Chapter 4

After The Flood

Devotion

Have your Bible, a journal and pen handy. Look up the verses quoted. Read them, the verses around them, and write down what you learn.

When God came down to stop the people from building their city and their tower, we must understand He wasn't against building cities or nice buildings. He helped David establish the city of Jerusalem. He helped Solomon build his palace and the beautiful grand Temple in Jerusalem. What God saw on the plains of Shinar was the people's rebellion to His command and authority.

Genesis 11:4 states, "And they said, Come, let us build a city and a tower with its head in the heavens, and make a name for ourselves, that we not be scattered on the face of all the earth." Making a name for yourself may seem harmless. We think of it as being successful. The key word in this verse, however, is "selves." (LITV)

The Hebrew word translated name means more than successful. It can also mean authority. The Hebrew word is used several times in the

Bible in reference to reputation. Reputation is your overall character as judged or recognized by others.

When we read Genesis 11:4, we must remember how it relates to the earlier part of Noah's account after he left the ark in Genesis 9. We call this reading a verse in its context. God told Noah and his sons to be fruitful, to multiply and to fill the earth. They were to spread out on the earth while maintaining a bond with each other. The first part of the command they seemed to be doing. The population was increasing. But in Genesis 11:4 we can see their reluctance to "fill" the earth.

They did not want to be scattered. The meaning is literally broken in pieces. Some scholars wonder where they got the idea that moving about the earth would break their relationship with each other? Were they already experiencing arguments that brought divisions? Others point out it was their unity that got them into trouble.

Whatever their reasons, Genesis 11:4 shows their fear and their solution for it. They decided to be their own authority and make up their own rules. The tower would be the symbol to unite them and create their reputation and identity.

But why would they need an outward symbol if they were united in their hearts to one another? Why couldn't their unity be in God and praise to Him? Why couldn't their building be in honor of Him?

All these questions reveal something was not quite right with the motives of these people. What was uniting them was their rebellion against God. The tower was their rallying cry for defiance. Every time one of them looked up at it, it would remind them of who they wanted to be and what their purpose was. This would bring them fame and bring the reputation they desired. It sounds a lot like the people living before the flood, doesn't it?

There are many people who still have the same desires and dreams today. King Solomon was one of the most successful kings of ancient Israel. He wrote about how to be successful God's way. One thing he said was, "Entrust your work to the LORD, and your planning will succeed." (Proverbs 16:3 ISV) His father was King David, another successful king of Israel. He wrote, "Commit thy way unto the LORD; trust also in him; and he shall bring it to pass." (Psalms 37:5)

But the people building the tower trusted in themselves and in the demons they decided to honor with their worship. They committed themselves to this goal, and God hindered it. When He changed the language from one to several, He made it easier for people to separate from each other. It didn't stop them from worshipping demons, however.

Committing your way to God means rolling the care of it upon God. When you do this, He will help you succeed. We may think we know how to do something the right way, but God is the only one who knows all the details and stumbling blocks in front of us. When our desire is to honor Him, His desire is to help us.

Drawing Near Activity: Answer the questions below.
What goals do you have?

How do they honor God?

If your goals do not honor God, what changes do you need to make so that they can?

You can ask God to give you desires that agree with His plans and ones He can bless. As you do your part to achieve your goals, trust God that he will do His. Start praising Him for success. As you honor Him, He will honor you.

Chapter 4 General Questions

1. If Genesis 7:11 tells us when the flood began, why are we not sure when it started?

2. How many days and nights did it rain?

3. What kind of rain was this and how do we know?

For Further Study:

There have been many major storms recorded in history. For example, one of the worst in the United States happened in Galveston, Texas on September 8, 1900, when a hurricane killed an estimated 8,000 to 12,000 people.[1] In 1910 Paris, France saw heavy downpours that caused a flood lasting months.[2] In 1931, a flood covered a huge area in Central China killing 400,000 to around 4,000,000 people. Some died from the deadly diseases that followed, like typhus and cholera.[3] There were killing floods in England and Italy, and in 1993

---

[1] Elisha Fieldstadt. "Deadliest hurricanes in U.S. history." CBS News. August, 28, 2018. https://www.cbsnews.com/pictures/deadliest-hurricanes-worst-in-the-us-list/31/

[2] Hilary Brueck. "The heart of Paris is underwater — and the images are a shocking reminder that the city is unprepared." Business Insider. Jan 29, 2018 https://www.businessinsider.com/see-paris-underwater-as-the-seine-floods-the-streets-hundred-year-flood-2018-1#in-1910-the-river-crested-nine-feet-higher-than-todays-flood-levelssome-think-paris-is-disastrously-unprepared-for-another-flood-like-that-one-8

[3] Benjamin Elisha Sawe. "Worst Floods Recorded Since 1900." World Atlas. April 25, 2017. https://www.worldatlas.com/articles/worst-floods-recorded-since-1900.html

flooding continued for three months in the Midwest United States.[4] In 2022, twenty four inches of rain falling over three days caused major flooding in Brisbane, Australia.[5]

But what if that kind of rain fell for forty days? What if those kinds of storms lasted for a hundred days? What if the storm was worldwide?

As much damage as that kind of an event would cause, the flood of Noah's day was even worse. The ground broke apart. The ocean floor broke apart. Rain not only came from above. Water came from below.

Think of it. Can you imagine such a disaster? Nothing had ever happened like it, and nothing ever will again. God has promised.

4. According to Genesis 7:23 what happened to the people and things of the earth outside the ark?

5. How long did it take before the ark began to float?

6. How many days did it rain all together– in total?

7. What happened after the rain stopped?

---

[4] "Australia's 'rain bomb' and other deadly floods throughout history." LoveExploring. February 6, 2022. https://www.loveexploring.com/gallerylist/90532/the-worlds-worst-floods

[5] Renee Duff. "2 feet of rain leaves Australian city underwater." AccuWeather. February 27, 2022. https://www.accuweather.com/en/severe-weather/2-feet-of-rain-leaves-australian-city-underwater/1149050

8. Where did the ark go aground?

9. What do we know about the land of Ararat?

10. Noah's ark has never been found. Where might it be located?

11. What method did Noah use to see if the water was receding?

12. How long were Noah and his family on the ark?

13. What process did Noah use to free the animals?

14. What was the land like outside the ark?

15. What is the Cradle of Civilization and why is it called that?

16. What is the Out of Africa theory?

17. What are some problems with the Out of Africa theory?

18. What ancient site interests scholars who believe the Bible and why?

19. What is the first thing Noah did when he left the ark?

20. What did God tell Noah about the animals?

21. What are the new rules God gave Noah?

22. What command was missing?

23. Did Noah and his sons have to learn to use tools?

24. Why were their first homes so primitive?

25. Noah was six hundred years old when the flood started. How many more years did he live after the flood?

26. What work did Noah do after he left the ark?

27. Why did Noah curse Ham's son Canaan?

28. What else do we know about Canaan?

29. Who is Eber and why did he name his son Peleg?

30. How did the people who gathered on the plains of Shinar disobey God?

31. How did the people know how to make bricks and how was their method different than people who lived later?

32. What does this method of brick-making tell us about the building they were constructing?

33. What is the traditional name for this building?

34. What do we think this structure looked like?

35. What was God's response to the people's building project?

36. Is there any archaeological evidence pointing to the beginning of different languages?

37. What does the account of the Tower of Babel explain?

38. How many language roots are there and where did many of them begin?

For further study:

It is debated by scientists how language began. Some do not believe man could have invented language because then he would have had to understand how to use a language and have been using one already. Others think sign language came first. Still others think language developed gradually. The problem is there is no evidence for any of these theories— which, linguists are quick to admit. A linguist is one who studies speech and languages.

Scientists believe that man's capability for speech is because his larynx is situated lower in his throat than a monkey's larynx. They think this lower larynx happened about 300,000 years ago. Earlier men couldn't speak. But somehow the larynx dropped lower, grew lower and voilà! Man started talking. This is called the LDT theory for laryngeal descent theory.[6]

---

[6] Rachel Gutman "A 'Mic Drop' on a Theory of Language Evolution." *The Atlantic*. Dec 12, 2019. https://www.theatlantic.com/science/archive/2019/12/when-did-ancient-humans-start-speak/603484/

Recently a new theory has been introduced that states man could speak as early as 27 million years ago.[7] The scientists who agree with this theory believe the anatomy of man's throat was already formed by that date. The only problem? None of it can be proved. All the components of the throat they need to study are soft tissues. But soft tissue rots after a person dies.[8] Still, they think man has been talking for a *really* long time.

Something else interesting to our study is what linguists have discovered about shared words. Ida Eriksen reported in her article for *ScienceNordic* that "Linguists have found words that have similar sounds in various languages." [9] Over 6,000 languages have been studied. Some words have similar sounds and meanings.

But questioning minds are stirring disagreement in the ranks of science. One question is what else has man got that monkeys don't? Another is why are man's speech capabilities unique to him? According to the Linguistic Society of America, "This issue is particularly controversial."[10]

What might different languages with shared sounds and meanings indicate? Why do you think questions about man's unique ability to speak are troublesome?

Activity: Compare greetings like hello or the words for goodbye in

[7] Ibid.

[8] Ibid.

[9] Ida Eriksen. "Two-thirds of all languages use similar sounds in common words," *ScienceNordic.* October21, 2016. https://sciencenordic.com/denmark-language-society--culture/two-thirds-of-all-languages-use-similar-sounds-in-common-words/1438756

[10] Linguistic Society of America FAQ: How Did Language Begin? https://www.linguisticsociety.org/resource/faq-how-did-language-begin

French, Italian, Portuguese, English, German and Spanish. You can use an online translation service if you are able to access the internet. Listen to their pronunciations. Write them down. Now find the same greetings in Hungarian. Do they sound similar? Using the same languages, find the word for water. Continue to compare languages. Are there any you think might be related?

Activity: Read pages 58-59 again. Explain how the human genome and the study of DNA support the account of Genesis and the Table of Nations in Genesis 10.

39. What does people speaking similar languages tell us about them?

40. Why is unity called a tool?

Chapter Evaluation

Student may write what they learned from this chapter, using a paragraph essay format. Suggested: 500 words or one page. Alternative: Student may give an oral report or Charlotte Mason style narration. Or student may complete the test provided below.

Chapter 4 Test 1

1. If Genesis 7:11 tells us when the flood began, why are we not sure when it started?

2. How many days and nights did it rain?

3. According to Genesis 7:23 what happened to the people and things of the earth outside the ark?

4. How many days did it rain all together– in total?

5. How long were Noah and his family on the ark?

6. What was the land like outside the ark?

7. What is the Out of Africa theory and what are some problems with this theory?

8. When God gave Noah His new rules what command was missing and why?

9. What ancient site interests scholars who believe the Bible and why?

10. What is the first thing Noah did when he left the ark?

Chapter 4 Test 2

1. Did Noah and his sons have to learn to use tools?

2. Why were their first homes so primitive?

3. What else do we know about Canaan?

4. Who is Eber and why did he name his son Peleg?

5. How did the people know how to make bricks and how was their method different than people who lived later? What does this method of brick-making tell us about the building they were constructing?

6. Why did the people of Shinar build a tower and what do we think this structure looked like?

7. Is there any archaeological evidence pointing to the beginning of different languages?

8. What does the account of the Tower of Babel explain?

9. How many language roots are there and where did many of them begin?

10. What does people speaking similar languages tell us about them?

• Chapter 5 •

Flood Stories

Devotion

Have your Bible, a journal and pen handy. Look up the verses quoted. Read them, the verses around them, and write down what you learn.

Don Richardson was a missionary to the Sawi people in New Guinea. He wrote a book about his experiences called *Peace Child*. He and his wife and his seventh month old son went to live among the Sawi in 1962. The Sawi people were violent cannibals. The Richardsons lived among them safely for years, but they began to wonder if the Sawi would ever receive Jesus as their Savior.

When Don told them the story of Jesus they were so excited they cheered. Don was surprised until he realized they were excited about Judas, the man who betrayed Jesus with a kiss. Judas was their hero because they honored deceit and practiced it against each other. They called Judas a Master of Treachery and wanted to know more about him.

One day, Don Richardson told them if they did not stop fighting with the neighboring villages, he was going to leave. The Sawi did not want them to leave. Don's wife was a nurse and had saved so many Sawi lives they called her The Woman Who Makes All The Villages Well.

The Sawi tried to explain that making peace was not an easy thing to do. They had slaughtered their enemies and committed horrific crimes against one another. Don didn't understand their reluctance. He urged them to make peace.

The Sawi did have one way to make a peace treaty. One father had to agree to give his child to another father from the other tribe to raise as a peace child. The tradition required one father to give a son to his enemy. This he would have to do at great risk. Since deceit was one of their values, one tribe could be setting a trap for the other.

One Sawi father in Don Richardson's village understood how serious the situation was. But he was the only father willing to give his son to the other tribe. It was a great sacrifice. He had only one child. The other village was amazed that this man would give his only son to them to be the peace child. Young and old in the tribe touched the baby, receiving him as the way to peace.

Don was stunned. He hadn't understood this is what peace required of them. But here, hidden in their culture, was the opening he needed to share Jesus as God's only Son, the real Peace Child.

Ancient Egyptians were focused on sin and death. Judgment was a big theme in their burial rituals. In the Hindu culture the way to be healed is to be born again. They understand this happens through dying and coming to life again as another person (reincarnation). Hindus also have a festival (Diwali) that celebrates light triumphing over darkness, good over evil. Do you see anything special about these things compared to the story of Jesus?

These are just some examples of truths that are embedded in other cultures. When they are discovered, they give missionaries a way to share the Good News of Jesus. Don Richardson said God has been at work planting these seeds of truth.

Drawing Near Activity:

Not only are there language and flood stories throughout the earth, but there are beliefs, traditions and words hidden in cultures that reflect truths to share Jesus. Consider God the Father, who so wants people to accept His love that He has worked to create paths He can use to teach them about His Son Jesus. God's desire is mercy. He is love. What does that mean to you? Take the time right now to consider all the ways God gives you His love. Make a list and thank Him for each one.

Chapter 5 General Questions

1. Who is George Smith and what is one of his achievements?

2. Is there any other ancient literature besides the Bible that tells the story of the Tower of Babel? If so, name one.

3. Where can Tower and language legends be found?

4. What is a myth?

5. What is an etiological myth?

6. What is a legend?

7. How do we decide what is a myth and what is a legend?

8. Where can flood myths be found?

9. What do you think is important about flood myths?

10. Describe the two versions of the Babylonian story called the *Atrahasis Epic*.

11. What is the most famous Babylonian flood story?

12. Who was Hormuzd Rassam?

13. Tell about Rassam's discovery.

For Further Study:

Did you ever wish you could meet one of the people from Ninevah who heard Jonah preach to them? What would it have been like to listen to a man who had been barfed up by a whale say you had better listen to God and repent? He would get your attention wouldn't he?

Well the people of Ninevah listened. They became the first believers in Ninevah and passed their faith down to generation after generation of Ninevites. There have been Christians living in that town ever since recent times. In fact, Hormuzd Rassam was one of those Christians.

You see Ninevah is today's Mosul, Iraq. It is part of Iraqi Kurdistan. But ISIS destroyed the city and persecuted the Christians living there. Today it is still in ruins.

Hormuzd Rassam would be very sad. Mosul was his home. He was born there in 1826, and his family worshipped in a church there.

When he was nineteen, Rassam worked as an assistant to the famous archaeologist Austen Henry Layard. After Layard became ill and returned to Britain, Rassam continued to excavate in Mosul. He was in his twenties, working in his hometown, and he had an instinct that helped him find ancient Assyrian treasures.

Rassam became Iraq's first archaeologist. He discovered several important finds including bronze gates and thousands of tablets and cylinders. Rassam wrote about his adventures in his book, *Asshur and the Land of Nimrod.*[1]

Even though Rassam made great discoveries, such as the relief showing Sennacherib's siege of Lachish told in 2Chronicles 32, he was never given the respect or honor he deserved. Instead, some considered him a treasure hunter. All of his discoveries, however, were received by the British Museum. You can see them there today.

Later he married an English woman and lived near London. The British asked him to go to Ethiopia to help free British missionaries there. He went and ended up being put in prison too. He was freed two years later when the British fought the Battle of Magdala.[2]

If you would like, you can read Rassam's book online on the Internet Archive website.

14. Who translated the tablets known as the *Epic of Gilgamesh*?

---

[1] Jane Waldron Grutz. "Iraq's First Archeologist." AramcoWorld. May/June 2018. https://www.aramcoworld.com/Articles/May-2018/Iraq-s-First-Archeologist

[2] Esther Lang. "Hormuzd Rassam." Assyrian Cultural Foundation. July 30. https://www.auaf.us/blog/hormuzd-rassam/

15. Are the *Atrahasis Epic* and the *Epic of Gilgamesh* original stories?

16. Who was Gilgamesh and what did he do?

17. In your own words tell the story of the *Epic of Gilgamesh.*

18. Why does Nozomi Osanai believe the Genesis account of the flood is the original account?

19. Who are the Miao people and why is their flood story amazing?

20. What are geological evidences for the flood?

21. How are fossils formed?

22. How do jellyfish point to a worldwide flood?

23. Describe the K-T event.

24. Compare the evolutionists' view of the geologic column with Dr. Andrew Snelling's view.

25. Could any of the layers of the geological column have happened slowly?

26. What did Darwin realize?

27. Who was Melchizedek and why is he important to our study?

Activity: Read Ephesians 4:17-18, and then write it your own words.

28. What does *mataiotēs* mean?

29. What is our understanding like when we separate from God?

30. What lesson can we learn from the Miao people?

Chapter Evaluation

Student may write what they learned from this chapter, using a paragraph essay format. Suggested: 500 words or one page. Alternative: Student may give an oral report or Charlotte Mason style narration. Or student may complete the test provided below.

Chapter 5 Test

1. Is there any other ancient literature besides the Bible that tells the story of the Tower of Babel? If so, name one.

2. Where can Tower, flood and language legends be found?

3. What is an etiological myth?

4. Are the *Atrahasis Epic* and the *Epic of Gilgamesh* original stories?

5. Why does Nozomi Osanai believe the Genesis account of the flood is the original account?

6. How do jellyfish point to a worldwide flood?

7. Compare the evolutionists' view of the geologic column with Dr. Andrew Snelling's view.

8. Could any of the layers of the geological column have happened slowly?

9. What did Darwin realize?

10. Who was Melchizedek and why is he important to our study?

Chapter 6

City Builders

Devotion

Have your Bible, a journal and pen handy. Look up the verses quoted. Read them, the verses around them, and write down what you learn.

Dr. Nathaniel Jeanson is a scientist and researcher who has written a book called *Traced: Human DNA's Big Surprise*. It has been described as a ground breaking book. Jeanson traces human history using DNA back to Noah's sons. Are you related to Ham, Shem or Japheth? You'll have to read the book to find the answer and brace yourself to be amazed.

DNA is our unique fingerprint. That is unless you have an identical twin. Or your blood is completely replaced with someone else's.

That is what happened to one pastor's grandson. The little boy's blood was so diseased it needed to be replaced down to the last drop. Fortunately, his brother was a perfect match. Before the procedure was completed, the doctor told the young boy it would be the last time he would talk to him as he was. The next day he would be a brand new person. In fact, if his brother ever committed a crime, he could be blamed for it if police tested his DNA.

When we ask Jesus into our heart, it is a bit like changing our DNA. But it is our spiritual DNA that changes. Jesus blood changes us on the inside in our spirit. The process also changes our position. Before we asked Jesus into our heart, we were not a child of God, seated in heaven with authority over satan. But when we become a child of God, God gives us this place of authority over our enemy satan. Even a five-year-old who accepts Jesus as his Savior and Lord can resist satan and he has to leave.

In this chapter we have learned about ancient people who built cities. One day you might be a city builder too. But the most important thing to build is your relationship with Jesus. We are to walk with Him like people walked with God in the Old Testament. Colossians 2:6-7 says, "As ye have therefore received Christ Jesus the Lord, so walk ye in him: Rooted and built up in him, and established in the faith, as ye have been taught, abounding therein with thanksgiving."

Jesus also wants to give us a Helper called Holy Spirit. He is responsible for guiding you every day and being your Teacher. Of course, you have to let Him do this.

Once you have asked Jesus into your heart, you can ask Holy Spirit to fill you up on the inside. Jesus also called Him the Comforter. "But when the Comforter is come, whom I will send unto you from the Father, even the Spirit of truth, which proceedeth from the Father, he shall testify of me." (John 15:26)

Jesus said Holy Spirit will teach you. "...when he, the Spirit of truth, is come, he will guide you into all truth: for he shall not speak of himself; but whatsoever he shall hear, that shall he speak: and he will shew you things to come. He shall glorify me: for he shall receive of mine, and shall shew it unto you." (John 16:13-14)

Noah and the people of the Old Testament could not ask Jesus or Holy Spirit to live inside them. We are living in the time they hoped for. God did everything He could to give us His love. Jesus gave everything He possessed to give us this new life and position. Because They did this, we should receive everything They've done.

The kind of world you see around you based on the world's wisdom is not the world God has prepared for you to live in forever. Noah's 8th great grandson was Abraham. He was a man who walked by faith in a land God was going to give him. But Abraham built no cities in that land. Instead, he built altars. Hebrews 11:10 says this about him: "... he looked for a city which hath foundations, whose builder and maker is God."

If we are careful to build our lives on God's words and His ways, if we build ourselves up by leaning on Jesus and Holy Spirit, someday we will see that heavenly city Abraham looked forward to.

Drawing Near Activity: Here is a prayer you can speak over yourself everyday.

"For this cause we also, since the day we heard it, do not cease to pray for you, and to desire that ye might be filled with the knowledge of his will in all wisdom and spiritual understanding; That ye might walk worthy of the Lord unto all pleasing, being fruitful in every good work, and increasing in the knowledge of God; Strengthened with all might, according to his glorious power, unto all patience and longsuffering with joyfulness; Giving thanks unto the Father, which hath made us meet to be partakers of the inheritance of the saints in light: Who hath delivered us from the power of darkness, and hath translated us into the kingdom of his dear Son: In whom we have redemption through his blood, even the forgiveness of sins." (Colossians 1:9-14)

You can personalize it like this:

Thank You Lord that I am being filled with the knowledge of Your will through all wisdom and spiritual understanding so that I walk worthy of You, pleasing You, being fruitful and successful in every good work. Thank You that I am increasing in the knowledge of You, being strengthened with all Your glorious power so that I can endure with joy. I give You thanks for making me right with You so that I can inherit what You have given Your people. Thank You for delivering me from the power of darkness and moving me into the kingdom of Jesus Your dear Son. In Jesus I have been made clean through His blood. I am forgiven.

Write this on a 3x5 card or note paper and put it in a place where you will remember to speak it everyday.

Chapter 6 General Questions

1. Name some ziggurats you can visit in the Middle East and tell where they are located.

2. How long does it take to walk around the foundation of the Great Ziggurat in Iraq?

3. What were ziggurats used for?

4. What is the *Enuma Elish* and what do some scholars think it shows us about the people living after the flood?

5. What might the eight kings listed on the Sumerian King List show us?

6. What kind of religion did the people of Babylon develop?

For Further Study:

The Annunaki gods may have been inspired by the eight kings identified on the Sumerian King List, but they were the false gods called the Mesopotamian Pantheon. The Mesopotamian gods were worshipped by ancient Sumerians, Akkadians, Babylonians, Armenians and the Canaanites of the Bible. They are featured in ancient literature like *Enki and the World Order*. In this story, Enki calls himself the self reliant father who was birthed by a bull and is the "great dragon who stands in Eridug," one of the Anuna gods.[1]

Another source is *Inana's Descent into the Netherworld*. This story is about Inana abandoning heaven and earth and going into the underworld to rule it. It was a dangerous place of death and she asked her worshippers to cut themselves while they prayed for her.[2]

These gods were said to be powerful heavenly beings before they were associated with the underworld. Although this pantheon changed with time, it included Enki, Enlil, Inana, An, Ninhursag and Utu. Many of these were gods at Eridu. One of the gods was Marduke who was a chief god in Babylon. The Bible mentions Marduke as one of the pagan gods sinful people worshipped.

According to archaeologists Dr. Jeremy Black and Dr. Anthony Green in their book, *Gods, Demons and Symbols of Ancient Mesopotamia: An Illustrated Dictionary*, the Babylonians described these gods as wearing a substance called melam, a type of light and terrifying splendor.[3] This light seemed to ooze from gods, kings, pagan temples and idols. Ancient sources state when a person saw melam or experienced

---

[1] J.A. Black, G. Cunningham, E Fluckiger-Hawker, E. Robson, and G. Zólyomi, The Electronic Text Corpus of Sumerian Literature (http://www-etcsl.orient.ox.ac.uk/), Oxford 1998- https://etcsl.orinst.ox.ac.uk/section1/tr113.htm.

[2] J.A. Black, G. Cunningham, E Fluckiger-Hawker, E. Robson, and G. Zólyomi, The Electronic Text Corpus of Sumerian Literature (http://www-etcsl.orient.ox.ac.uk/), Oxford 1998-

[3] Jeremy Black and Anthony Green. *Gods, Demons and Symbols of Ancient Mesopotamia: An Illustrated Dictionary*, (London, England: The British Museum Press, 1992), 93-94. https://www.academia.edu/4845062/AN_ILLUSTRATED_DICTIONARY_Gods_Demons_and_Symbols_of_Ancient_Mesopotamia

its effect, it caused their flesh to tingle or creep. Ni is a word the Babylonians used to describe the effect. Ni means fear.[4]

The Eight Immortals in Chinese mythology is another adaptation of these false gods. There are theories these Annunaki gods were aliens, and books and movies portray theories about them.

Did you notice the clues that point to the demon nature of this group of false gods? They were powerful heavenly beings that became associated with the underworld, the place of death, and wanted to rule it. They were clothed in a type of light that may have seemed glorious, but it didn't bring awe and a realization of the person's sin. They only felt fear. This light affected a person's flesh, the part of our nature that is carnal as taught in Romans 8.

One of the gods was Marduke, a god the Bible said not to worship. Enki is linked to another god who was a bull. The Bible talks about the Canaanites and the Egyptians worshipping false gods that were bulls. Enki calls himself a dragon, a creature the Bible links to satan in Revelation. Inana asked her worshippers to cut themselves which is like the pagan worship revealed in 1Kings 18:28 when Elijah confronted the priests of Baal.

All of these things are linked to satan and the worship of demons as idols. Deuteronomy 32:16-18 says, "You made God jealous and angry by worshiping disgusting idols and foreign gods. You offered sacrifices to demons, those useless gods that never helped you, new gods that your ancestors never worshiped. You turned away from God, your Creator; you forgot the Mighty Rock, the source of your life." (CEV)

The New Testament also says honoring false gods is worshipping

---

[4] Jeremy Black and Anthony Green. *Gods, Demons and Symbols of Ancient Mesopotamia: An Illustrated Dictionary*. 130 -131.

demons. "What say I then? that the idol is any thing, or that which is offered in sacrifice to idols is any thing? But I say, that the things which the Gentiles sacrifice, they sacrifice to devils, and not to God: and I would not that ye should have fellowship with devils." (1Corinthians 10:19-20) These demons are still popular as characters in games, books, videos and movies. They may have different names, but the same themes.

Considering this, why should we be careful of the types of games we play, books we read and shows or movies we watch? What can you do to protect yourself from these influences or when you are pressured to join in with your friends?

7. What word did Moses use to describe a ziggurat and why?

8. What do ziggurats reveal about the desire of the people who built them?

9. How is the God of the Bible different than the false gods the people worshipped?

10. Why couldn't the Tower of Babel be the ziggurat Nebuchadnezzar I or Nebuchadnezzar II built?

11. Does the Bible actually say Tower of Babel?

12. How many ziggurats do we know of in Mesopotamia?

Activity: Compare the step pyramids of Mesoamerica with the ziggurats in the Middle East. The biggest step pyramid is the Great Pyramid of Cholula in Puebla Mexico. The Pyramid of Kukulkan is a Mayan Temple. There are six step pyramids in Yalbac, Belize. Perhaps the most famous Mesoamerican ziggurat is an Aztec temple, the Pyramid of the Sun. Find a picture of it. What was it used for? Why are these Mesoamerican structures called step pyramids and the others ziggurats?

13. Who are the Halaf people?

14. Who are the Ubaid people and what was their culture like?

15. When did civilization begin?

16. Where did civilization begin after the flood?

17. What does *bâlal* mean?

18. What does the Bible reveal about the Shinar?

19. Who were the Sumerians?

20. What do we know about the Sumerian language?

21. Why is Eridu a good candidate for the city where the Tower of Babel is located?

22. Why are ziggurats found all over the earth?

23. What is the Uruk Expansion?

Activity: Draw a picture of the Uruk Expansion. What did the people look like? Dress like? What did they carry? What kind of homes did they build? What types of food did they eat? What might the children have been like? Draw your scene and share it with someone. Tell what you have learned about the Uruk Expansion.

24. What followed the forced separation at Babel?

25. Name some settlements that date to this period.

26. What do finds at Çatalhöyük and Ain Ghazal reveal?

27. Why did the Ohalo II village surprise the experts?

28. Why does it seem the ancient agricultural revolution burst on the scene in areas of Mesopotamia at the same time?

29. Who is Ötzi and what does he show us about the people living near the time of the Tower of Babel incident?

30. Why is the list in Genesis 10 called the Table of Nations important?

Chapter 6 Test

1. What is the *Enuma Elish* and what do some scholars think it shows us about the people living after the flood?

2. What word did Moses use to describe a ziggurat and why?

3. What do ziggurats reveal about the desire of the people who built them?

4. Why couldn't the Tower of Babel be the ziggurat Nebuchadnezzar I or Nebuchadnezzar II built?

5. Who were the Sumerians?

6. What do we know about the Sumerian language?

7. Why is Eridu a good candidate for the city where the Tower of Babel is located?

8. What is the Uruk Expansion?

9. Why does it seem the ancient agricultural revolution burst on the scene in areas of Mesopotamia at the same time?

10. Why is the list in Genesis 10 called the Table of Nations important?

Chapter 7

Empire Builders

Devotion

Have your Bible, a journal and pen handy. Look up the verses quoted. Read them, the verses around them, and write down what you learn.

According to archaeology, Gilgamesh was a real king. He went on a great journey, wrote a story and became famous. But there is another story in his tale.

He told us more about himself than what he wrote in words. Have you ever heard the expression you have to read between the lines? It means it is possible to understand someone's feelings, intentions or what is really happening without it being said.

In the *Epic of Gilgamesh*, Gilgamesh shows us he did not want to die. Was he afraid? He also lied about killing the gods of the forest. Even if Huwawa is not the God of the Bible, the bull of heaven was worshipped by various cultures and given various names until the time Israelites were taken to Babylon and after. An ungodly man like Gilgamesh was in no position to kill a demon god anyway.

Where is Gilgamesh today? Does his story change lives? Did it ever? Gilgamesh built his empire on lies he thought about himself. In reality, he had no power over demons or his own death.

Nimrod built his empire on lies too. They were the lies he thought about the world and based on the violent, deceitful values of pagan gods that were really demons. Nimrod is famous, but not for doing good.

Men build empires based on lies today.

• They build science empires on a lie about how the world began called evolution.

• They build history empires built on false information about mankind and true history.

• They build education empires built on a false view of what mankind should be and how he should act.

• They build religion empires on lies about God and what He is like.

What happens when you build an empire on a false foundation? In 1913 the Trancona grain elevator was built near Winnipeg, Canada. After it was finished, its tanks were filled with grain. Immediately workers saw settling of the building. In an hour it began to lean. In twenty-four hours the foundation collapsed.[1]

Jesus warned us to build on a firm foundation. He said that foundation is His word. We need to hear it, then do it.

"Therefore whosoever heareth these sayings of mine, and doeth them, I will liken him unto a wise man, which built his house upon a rock: And the rain descended, and the floods came, and the winds

---

[1] "A case of foundation soil failure – the Transcona grain elevator." Geotech. https://www.geotech.hr/en/case-of-foundation-soil-failure-transcona-grain-elevator/

blew, and beat upon that house; and it fell not: for it was founded upon a rock. And every one that heareth these sayings of mine, and doeth them not, shall be likened unto a foolish man, which built his house upon the sand: And the rain descended, and the floods came, and the winds blew, and beat upon that house; and it fell: and great was the fall of it." (Matthew 7:24-27)

Have you ever built a sandcastle on the beach? Is it still there? What happened to it?

That is what will happen to anything we build that doesn't agree with God's word. All the hard work we invested will be for nothing. But anything built on God's truth will stand.

In the first chapter's devotion we talked about knowledge and that wisdom is the ability to know how to use knowledge. Notice in the above verse Jesus calls the person who builds on the rock wise. Why? Because he knew what to do with the knowledge of God's word: practice it.

Drawing Near Activity: Take a moment and name things you should build on Jesus who is the Rock in the above parable. Examples are a marriage and a family. What else can you think of?

Here is a verse we have talked about in Chapter 6's devotion. "As ye have therefore received Christ Jesus the Lord, so walk ye in him: Rooted and built up in him, and established in the faith, as ye have been taught, abounding therein with thanksgiving." (Colossians 2:6-7)

This is the truth that if you practice it will help you avoid being fooled by people teaching false ideas as the passages next verse describes. "Beware lest any man spoil you through philosophy and vain deceit, after the tradition of men, after the rudiments of the world, and not after Christ." (Colossians 2:8)

Personalize the first section and speak it over yourself everyday. Below is a version you can copy on a 3x5 card if you would like.

I have received Jesus as my Savior and Lord; therefore I am walking in Him. I am being rooted and built up in Him. I am firmly fixed in my trust in Jesus. I am taught by Holy Spirit and I am overflowing with thanks to God.

Chapter 7 General Questions

1. What do we know about the Sumerian King List?

2. Why do some say there was a pre-Adamite civilization?

3. What does the Sumerian King List say about a flood?

4. What did Henry Rawlinson conclude about the Sumerians?

5. What type of government is described on the Sumerian King List?

6. What did scholars first think about the kings on the Sumerian King List?

7. Who was the first king to be identified as a real king?

8. What tower myth is connected to one of the kings on the List and what is the king's name?

9. Who is Gilgamesh and what is the name of his flood story?

10. According to his story, what was Gilgamesh like?

11. Who was Enkidu?

12. Briefly explain what happened in the Forest Journey.

13. Who do some scholars think Gilgamesh is in the Bible?

14. What does the Bible say about Nimrod and how does it describe him?

15. What does the word Nimrod mean?

16. What are the similarities between Nimrod and Gilgamesh?

17. What truths are hidden in the *Epic of Gilgamesh?*

18. What was Gilgamesh's purpose for writing the *Epic*?

19. How do we know Gilgamesh was a famous king?

20. If a man is known by his fruit, what might we conclude about Nimrod?

21. Is Gilgamesh Nimrod?

22. What is the most important thing to know about the *Epic of Gilgamesh*?

23. Does the Bible say Nimrod built the Tower of Babel?

24. What is the one ancient text we have that is whole and has guided archaeologists?

Activity: If we did not have the Bible as our guide, what might we think of the discoveries made by archaeologists? How would it change our view of history? If you never heard about a worldwide flood or a man named Noah, how would that change your understanding of the world? Ask someone else these same questions and write down what they say. Do you agree?

25. What followed Nimrod's city building efforts?

26. What does Dr. Johannes Krause's research tell us?

27. What is the most important thing to remember concerning evolutionists' theories about ancient man?

28. What are the problems with the evolutionists' timelines and charts for ancient man?

29. Briefly describe Noah's history before the flood and after.

Activity: If all the evidence for the accuracy of the Bible were presented to someone, would it guarantee they would accept the Bible as true and worth investigating for themselves? Why or why not? Imagine you are talking to this person, what would you say? Write it down and go over it. Take turns practicing with a believing friend. You will be ready to share what you know when you get the chance. Never be afraid to speak the truth about God or be discouraged if the person doesn't listen to you. You spoke and God will take it from there.

30. What is the major lesson Noah's life story teaches us?

Chapter Evaluation

Student may write what they learned from this chapter, using a paragraph essay format. Suggested: 500 words or one page. Alternative: Student may give an oral report or Charlotte Mason style narration. Or student may complete the test provided below.

Chapter 7 Test

1. Why do some say there was a pre-Adamite civilization?

2. What does the Sumerian King List say about a flood?

3. What tower myth is connected to one of the kings on the List and what is the king's name?

4. Who is Gilgamesh and what is the name of his flood story?

5. According to his story, what was Gilgamesh like?

6. What are the similarities between Nimrod and Gilgamesh?

7. What truths are hidden in the *Epic of Gilgamesh*?

8. What is the most important thing to know about the *Epic of Gilgamesh?*

9. What does Dr. Johannes Krause's research tell us?

10. What are the problems with the evolutionists' timelines and charts for ancient man?

Answer Keys

Lengthy answers are provided for some questions in order to give a complete answer for the instructor or to provide all possible answers. The student should answer according to their age level.

Chapter 1 General Questions

1. Who collected the histories and wrote them down in the book of Genesis? *Moses wrote them down while traveling around in the desert wilderness. pg 1*

2. When did man begin speaking a language? *Man was created speaking a language right away. On the day God made Adam, they were speaking to each other. (Gen 2:19) pg2*

3. What is a complex language? *Complex means the language uses words that can be arranged and connected to create meaning. pg 2*

4. What is evolutionists' theory about languages? *Their theory is simple languages grew more complex with time. pg 2*

5. What is the language principle? *It proves all living languages, the languages spoken today, are changing and becoming more simple. pg 3*

6. How old are languages and what is a Christian's reason for this approximate date? *Languages date back to 5,000 years or so. Christians view discoveries featuring ancient languages as the age men began multiplying again, after the flood. pg 3*

7. How many languages did people living directly after the flood speak? *The Bible makes it clear that all the people spoke one language before the flood and directly after. pg 4*

8. What is the oldest known alphabet? *According to Douglas Petrovich, the oldest know alphabet is Hebrew. pg 4*

109

9. Describe the discovery at Serabit el-Khadim? *Archaeological discoveries near the Sinai Desert's ancient turquoise mines show inscriptions at Serabit el-Khadim. They seem to be written by common laborers, probably slaves. This find shatters the idea that only scribes or educated people could write. pg 4-5*

10. What is the Bible's Hebrew storytelling method? *The Hebrew people had a system of repetition and storytelling tradition. First a general outline was given. Then more details were added. The system made it possible to keep accurate records. pg 5*

11. Is this method found outside the Bible? If yes, where? *Yes, this method is seen in archaeological discoveries like the Dead Sea Scrolls, the Copper Scrolls, the Silver Amulets and many other steles and monuments. pg 5*

12. What is the meaning of *towlĕdah* and how is the word used in the Bible? *Towlĕdah (toe-lay-DOTH) is the Hebrew word we translate as generations, and it means history or origin. The writers used it to say this is the history. pg 5*

13. Why are the Nuzi Tablets important to the family histories recorded in Genesis? *The Nuzi Tablets revealed over 5,000 family and government records. They showed family records were highly honored and kept, being passed down, father to son, for six generations. pg 5-6*

14. How long did people live in the era before the flood and after? *Early man lived for hundreds of years. pg 6*

Activity: Read Genesis 9:29 and Genesis 11:10 to Genesis 11: 32. Make a chart of the men's names and ages. What is the youngest recorded age of death before the flood? How long did Noah live? When did men begin to live shorter lives? *People living before the flood lived very long lives, living over 900 years. The youngest recorded age was 777. Noah lived 959 years. After the flood men began living shorter lives. For example, Shem lived 500 years but his son lived 400 years, and so it went until the average lifespan was around 200 years at the time of Peleg.*

15. Why is man not equal to animals? *Man is the only creation He made in His image. Man is also the only creation God breathed His DNA into, and the only one He gave dominion over the rest of creation. pg 6-7*

For Further Study: Read Psalm 8. In Psalm 8:5 the word translated angels in most Bibles are the Hebrew *min* (part of; from; out of) and *'ĕlôhîym* (a word used for the Supreme God). Green's *Literal Translation of the Bible* reads, "For You have made him lack a little from God; and have crowned him with glory and honor." Now read the chapter again. How does this change your understanding of the Psalm? What does this verse mean to you? *Answers will vary.*

16. How might the story of creation been recorded? *God told Adam and he wrote it down. pg 7*

17. Does the Bible support an old earth? *The Bible does not support an old earth. You have to go outside the Bible to claim the world was created in billions of years. The Hebrew word yom means day, and the writers further explained a twenty-four hour day by including the words evening ('ereb) and morning (bôqer). pg 7-8*

18. Describe the Garden of Eden. Where might it be? *A mist came from the ground every night to water the plants and trees. A river flowed through the land and also provided water. This river separated into four rivers. These rivers are the Tigris, Euphrates, Pishon and Gihon. The land of Havilah had gold and precious gems. While we don't know for sure, Moses' description seems to include Israel's boundaries. pg 8-9*

19. Does the Bible tell us about all of Adam's sons? *The Bible does not give us detailed information of all of Adam's children. pg 9-10*

20. Who was Cain and what was he like? *Cain was Adam's son. Cain had a bad attitude about bringing sacrifices to God. He did not do what was best. It made him angry when God accepted his brother Abel's sacrifice and not his. When God spoke to him about changing his attitude, Cain became angry. He did not want to change his behavior or his attitude.*

He killed Abel and then had to leave the place where his father and other brothers and sisters were living. pg 10

21. Who was Lucifer and what was his plan? *Lucifer was one of God's angels who rebelled against God. He wanted to be like God. He wanted to trick Adam into giving him the rule of the earth and everything in it. pg 10*

22. What didn't Adam and Eve know about? *They didn't know about evil which included sin and sickness. pg 11*

23. Was Adam deceived? *Eve was deceived. Adam was not. 1 Timothy 2:14 says "And Adam was not deceived, but the woman being deceived was in the transgression." pg 12*

24. What didn't Adam realize before he decided to disobey God? *Adam did not realize the consequence of his decision, that Lucifer would take away his dominion. pg 12*

25. Why did Adam and Eve have to leave the Garden? *Since Adam and Eve lost their right to rule, they had to leave the Garden. God told Adam under Lucifer's rule life would not be easy. His life became hard, and all the earth was affected. No longer could they eat from the Tree of Life. pg 12*

26. When Cain sinned and killed Abel how might it have reminded Adam of his sin? *When Cain committed his horrible crime, Adam may have remembered the day of his own sin and how he had to leave the garden God had made for him. It must have grieved him that it was his fault Lucifer's rebellion had taken over earth. pg 12*

27. Why did God want the creation account and Adam's history written down? *God wanted these things written so we would know our Creator and how the earth and all it contains came to be. He also wanted us to know our place in the world. God wanted us to know how special we are out of all His creation, that we are the only beings created in His likeness, a spirit being. pg 12-13*

28. What else did God give man when He created him that gives man the ability to choose? *God gave us freedom to make our own decisions. pg 13*

29. How does sin influence our world? *It can be seen in nature when animals kill each other, in harsh weather and disasters. It is the cause of disease in every living thing, of hatred and death. It is the cause of people being poor and starving. pg 13*

30. What are the two deaths Adam and Eve experienced? *They experienced a spiritual death first and a physical death later. pg 13*

31. What was God's promise to Adam and Eve after they had sinned? *God promised to send them a Deliverer who would save them from their sin predicament. pg 14*

32. How many years passed before this promise was fulfilled? *Four thousand years passed before Jesus was born into the world. pg 14*

33. Who was the Deliverer? *Jesus was the promised Deliverer. pg 14*

34. List the things Noah knew.
- *Man could speak*
- *Man could write*
- *Man lived long lives*
- *Man was created*
- *Man betrayed God*
- *Noah knew the result of man's betrayal*
- *Noah knew the promise of a Deliverer who would bring rest pg 1-14*

35. What is the gift called that God provided through His Deliverer?

We call this gift salvation because it saves us from punishment and all the bad things Satan can do to us. pg 15

Chapter 1 Test Answers

1. When did man begin speaking a language? *Man was created speaking a language right away. On the day God made Adam, they were speaking to each other. (Gen 2:19) pg2*

2. What is evolutionists' theory about languages? *Their theory is simple languages grew more complex with time. pg 2*

3. What is the language principle? *It proves all living languages, the languages spoken today, are changing and becoming more simple. pg 3*

4. How old are languages and what is a Christian's reason for this approximate date? *Languages date back to 5,000 years or so. Christians view discoveries featuring ancient languages as the age men began multiplying again, after the flood. pg 3*

5. What is the oldest known alphabet? *According to Douglas Petrovich, the oldest know alphabet is Hebrew. pg 4*

6. What is the Bible's Hebrew storytelling method? *The Hebrew people had a system of repetition and storytelling tradition. First a general outline was given. Then more details were added. The system made it possible to keep accurate records. pg 5*

7. What is the meaning of *towlĕdah* and how is the word used in the Bible? *Towlĕdah (toe-lay-DOTH) is the Hebrew word we translate as generations, and it means history or origin. The writers used it to say this is the history. pg 5*

8. Why are the Nuzi Tablets important to the family histories recorded in Genesis? *The Nuzi Tablets revealed over 5,000 family and government records. They showed family records were highly honored and kept, being passed down, father to son, for six generations. pg 5-6*

9. What are the two deaths Adam and Eve experienced? *They experi-*

enced a spiritual death first and a physical death later. pg 13

10. List the things Noah knew.
- *Man could speak*
- *Man could write*
- *Man lived long lives*
- *Man was created*
- *Man betrayed God*
- *Noah knew the result of man's betrayal*
- *Noah knew the promise of a Deliverer who would bring rest pg*

1-14

Chapter 2 General Questions

1. What is the Gap Theory of creation? *Some scholars believe there is a gap of time between the verses of Genesis 1:1-2. They think dinosaurs lived in these gap years for thousands of years. Some think men lived in this gap too. pg 17-18*

2. What is the age of time the Bible tells us about? *The only age we know for certain is ours. Genesis tells about our beginnings. Revelation tells how our age will end, and it gives us a glimpse of our future life. pg 18*

3. When did James Ussher and others think the earth was created? *They all agreed that creation happened around four thousand BC, give or take a few years. pg 18*

4. What did Cain do after he had to leave the area where Adam and Eve were living? *Cain moved away and built a city. He named the town after one of his sons, Enoch. pg 19*

5. What did Antonio Snider-Pellegrini discover? *In 1859, Antonio Snider-Pellegrini realized four of the continents we see today fit together like puzzle pieces. When he read Genesis 1:9-10, he understood it as God creating one huge section of land. pg 19-20*

6. What is a Super Continent? *God created one huge section of land. We call this a Super Continent. pg 20*

7. Is Snider-Pellegrini's theory accepted? *Snider-Pellegrini's theory is generally accepted, but his drawing of the land mass is not. pg 20*

8. What is the name of Snider-Pellegrini's map? *Snider-Pellegrini's map is called Pangaea (pan-JEE-yah). pg 20*

9. How do geologists know where the continents fit together? *Geologists study the rock layers along the edges of the continents to compare them. What they find are sediment layers on top, the scattered waste of dead plants and animals from the flood, and pure, original rock below. (The original rock is called craton or basement rock.) When similarities are discovered, it helps them determine the edges of the puzzle pieces. pg 20*

10. What is the name given to the map geologists agree on? *Their drawing is called Rodinia (roh-DEEN-ee-yah). pg 20*

11. Are these maps perfectly reliable? *No. Putting all the little pieces together is not easy because there is more than one way to do it. We cannot look at a map of Rodinia in perfect confidence. pg 20*

12. Describe what the Super Continent was like. *Noah's world had land all in one piece in some shape with the oceans around it. There were grasslands and forests. Some of these forests were tropical-type forests with large palms and ferns. In the pre-flood world of Noah there were evergreen trees and bushes, those that had flowers and those that lost their leaves. There were groundcovers and vines, some that flowered and some that had thorns. Plant-eating animals like giraffes, elephants, deer, dinosaurs, rabbits, sheep, rodents and monkeys lived on this land. Meat-eating animals roamed there too like large cats, small cats, bears, other dinosaurs and wolves. Small birds, large birds, including flying reptiles like the pterodactyl, and bats flew overhead or stood in marshes. The ocean was filled with plant life, whales, sharks, swimming dinosaurs, fish large and small, crabs*

and other crustaceans and shellfish. There were fungi and bacteria, insects and spiders. Most of these did not look exactly like modern mammals, birds and insects, however. The pre-flood world had a mild climate, allowing life to flourish. It is believed there were no vast mountain ranges. pg20-22

13. What does fossilized tree resin tell us about the earth's temperature? *Fossilized tree resins have shown the world was warmer. pg20-21*

14. What creatures did Noah take with him on the ark? *Noah did not take every species with him on the ark. He took only male and female kinds of every type of land creature. pg21*

15. How many people do we estimate were on the earth in Noah's time? *In Noah's day it is estimated there were around 750 million people. Some guess four billion because of the ancients' long life-spans and the chance to have lots of kids. pg 22*

16. What did ancient people look like? *Creationists do not believe man looked like an ape or a chimp. Geneticists say Adam and Eve had medium brown skin with brown eyes and hair. This would supply the genes necessary for all the variations we see today. We can be assured people looked like people. pg 22-23*

17. Who is Cheddar Man? *Cheddar Man is named for where his skeleton was found near Cheddar Gorge in southwest England. Recent DNA testing amazed scientists when they discovered he had dark skin, blue eyes and black curly hair. They expected light skin and fair hair. pg 22*

18. What are theories about Cheddar Man and why does scientist

Mark Thomas disagree? *They think Cheddar Man traveled from Africa to the Middle East before going to England. One theory from the study of Cheddar Man is that light skin developed because there is less sun in the north. About this scientist Mark Thomas says, "But it doesn't explain eye pigmentation. There are other processes that go on. It could be sexual selection. It could even be something else we don't yet understand." pg 22*

For Further Study: According to *Smithsonian Magazine,* Cheddar Man is the oldest complete skeleton discovered in England. The facial reconstruction of his image portrays him as a pleasant sort of guy. Even handsome in a rugged way. The important thing to notice is he looks like someone who could walk down a street in London today. But that is not what the scientists think, the scientists Mark Thomas disagrees with. Research Cheddar Man and find a picture of him. What do you think? Is he so different than someone you might meet today? *Answers will vary.*

19. Where do evolutionists think man began to live on the earth? *Africa. Evolutionists have painted a picture about ancient man that doesn't hold up against the evidence. They were positive they found the oldest human remains in Africa because this is where they believe man began. Close to apes. But scores of discoveries are proving their theories wrong. Even their dates for man. Man, like the fossil forests, is older than they thought. Modern looking men. pg22-23*

20. What archaeological evidence upsets their theory? *Two skulls, one found in Morrocco and one in China, are alike. They are also older than*

anything found in Africa. In Qesem Cave in Israel a shocking discovery was made. It seems the cave was used as a type of school to teach people how to make flint tools and butcher animals. The real problem is this would mean they had to be smart enough to pass knowledge and be able to speak. They could make decisions, plan, sustain relationships and perform complex tasks and artistry. pg 23

21. What can we be sure of about ancient man? *We can be sure ancient man looked like modern man. pg 23*

22. Who was Lamech and what was he like? *Lamech was Cain's great-great-great-grandson. He did not honor God or God's ways. Lamech had two wives. He killed two men. pg 23*

23. What changed when Adam changed masters? *He was not like God on the inside anymore. pg 23*

24. Who was Enosh and what did people begin doing during his lifetime? *Cain had another brother named Seth. Enosh was one of Seth's sons. When Enosh was born, the Bible says men began calling on the name of the Lord. This means this was the time men began distinguishing themselves from those that did not honor God. pg24*

25. Describe the giants living in the pre-flood world and those living after. *Some men were strong and very tall. They were called giants and mighty men. A dragonfly with a two and a half foot wingspan, a spider with a twelve inch leg span, a rat weighing seven hundred pounds, a thirteen foot long armadillo and a twenty foot tall sloth are all scientifically accepted giants. pg 24*

26. What began to happen to the people living before the flood? (Gen 6:5) *They were becoming increasingly rebellious and violent. pg 24*

27. Who was Sanchuniathon and what was the world like that he wrote about? *He was a priest who had lived in Beirut, Lebanon perhaps around the time of Moses. Sanchuniathon wrote about the early history of the Phoenician religion and the ancient world before the flood. He wrote about farmers, shepherds, reed huts, brick-making and sons who made things from metal. He claimed they knew how to write before the flood. He said their gods were really humans who had died and then were worshipped as gods. Sanchuniathon described giants. He said people were so amazed at the bulk of these men they named mountains after them. He said women did not get married but had children with whomever they chose. This created siblings with different fathers. But there was no steady father to lead the family. It created mothers who thought little about properly caring for their children. He talked about nature worship and said Cain began this worship. People worshipped the sky, the wind, sun and stars. They believed creatures hatched from an egg and some became human. He talked about the beginnings of creation growing from putrid water. Some worshipped snakes because they saw them eating themselves. The circle of a snake eating itself reminded them of the cycle of life and death. Parents sacrificed their children to these gods. Murder was common. pg 25*

28. In Noah's world people lived very long lives. Is there archaeological evidence for this? *The Sumerian King List gives the names of eight kings before the flood and the years they reigned. The scribes who wrote the list recorded thousands of years for a king's lifespan. pg 26*

29. What is the problem with the Sumerian King List and how might

it be solved? *The problem is with the thousands of years. It may be that the scribes who wrote the history recorded the numbers using their number system which used 60 as a base. We still use a method of it to tell time on a clock. The Bible, however, counts years with a value of one. If the list is read making the changes, the King List and the Bible tell a similar story. Even if you do not make any changes, the Sumerian King List shows lifespans before the flood were long, and then grew shorter. Also the eight kings in the list represent eight generations. The Bible has ten. If you remove Adam and Noah, you have eight. These eight generations may represent the history after Adam until the flood. pg 26*

30. Briefly describe Noah's world. *The pre-flood world happened around six thousand years ago. There were a lot of intelligent but wicked people. Some of those people were big, giants even. All of the land was in one piece. An ocean surrounded it. The weather was calm and warm. Plants and animals flourished. It was not a world of complete chaos. There were cities and farms. Businessmen, craftsmen and musicians. People lived in reed huts and possibly brick homes. Men and women were getting married. Some not. They were having babies. Children were learning skills from adults. Adults taught other adults. There were some who worshipped God. There were those that worshipped dead people and nature. pg 27*

Chapter 2 Test Answers

1. When did James Ussher and others think the earth was created? *They all agreed that creation happened around four thousand BC, give or take a few years. pg 18*

2. What did Antonio Snider-Pellegrini discover? *In 1859, Antonio Snider-Pellegrini realized four of the continents we see today fit together like puzzle pieces. When he read Genesis 1:9-10, he understood it as God creating one huge section of land. pg 19-20*

3. What is a Super Continent? *God created one huge section of land. We call this a Super Continent. pg 20*

4. How do geologists know where the continents fit together and are their maps perfectly reliable? *Geologists study the rock layers along the edges of the continents to compare them. What they find are sediment layers on top, the scattered waste of dead plants and animals from the flood, and pure, original rock below. (The original rock is called craton or basement rock.) When similarities are discovered, it helps them determine the edges of the puzzle pieces. No, the maps are not reliable. Putting all the little pieces together is not easy because there is more than one way to do it. We cannot look at a map of Rodinia in perfect confidence. pg 20*

5. What does fossilized tree resin tell us about the earth's temperature? *Fossilized tree resins have shown the world was warmer. pg20-21*

6. Who is Cheddar Man? *Cheddar Man is named for where his skeleton was found near Cheddar Gorge in southwest England. Recent DNA test-*

ing amazed scientists when they discovered he had dark skin, blue eyes and black curly hair. They expected light skin and fair hair. pg 22

7. What are theories about Cheddar Man and why does scientist Mark Thomas disagree? *They think Cheddar Man traveled from Africa to the Middle East before going to England. One theory from the study of Cheddar Man is that light skin developed because there is less sun in the north. About this scientist Mark Thomas says, "But it doesn't explain eye pigmentation. There are other processes that go on. It could be sexual selection. It could even be something else we don't yet understand." pg 22*

8. Where do evolutionists think man began to live on the earth and what archaeological evidence upsets their theory? *Africa. Evolutionists have painted a picture about ancient man that doesn't hold up against the evidence. They were positive they found the oldest human remains in Africa because this is where they believe man began. Close to apes. But scores of discoveries are proving their theories wrong. Even their dates for man. Man, like the fossil forests, is older than they thought. Modern looking men. Two skulls, one found in Morrocco and one in China, are alike. They are also older than anything found in Africa. In Qesem Cave in Israel a shocking discovery was made. It seems the cave was used as a type of school to teach people how to make flint tools and butcher animals. The real problem is this would mean they had to be smart enough to pass knowledge and be able to speak. They could make decisions, plan, sustain relationships and perform complex tasks and artistry. pg 22- 23*

9. Who was Sanchuniathon and what was the world like that he wrote about? *He was a priest who had lived in Beirut, Lebanon perhaps around the time of Moses. Sanchuniathon wrote about the early history of the*

Phoenician religion and the ancient world before the flood. He wrote about farmers, shepherds, reed huts, brick-making and sons who made things from metal. He claimed they knew how to write before the flood. He said their gods were really humans who had died and then were worshipped as gods. Sanchuniathon described giants. He said people were so amazed at the bulk of these men they named mountains after them. He said women did not get married but had children with whomever they chose. This created siblings with different fathers. But there was no steady father to lead the family. It created mothers who thought little about properly caring for their children. He talked about nature worship and said Cain began this worship. People worshipped the sky, the wind, sun and stars. They believed creatures hatched from an egg and some became human. He talked about the beginnings of creation growing from putrid water. Some worshipped snakes because they saw them eating themselves. The circle of a snake eating itself reminded them of the cycle of life and death. Parents sacrificed their children to these gods. Murder was common. pg 25

10. In Noah's world people lived very long lives. Is there archaeological evidence for this? If so, is there a problem with it and how might it be solved? *The Sumerian King List gives the names of eight kings before the flood and the years they reigned. The scribes who wrote the list recorded thousands of years for a king's lifespan. The problem is with the thousands of years. It may be that the scribes who wrote the history recorded the numbers using their number system which used 60 as a base. We still use a method of it to tell time on a clock. The Bible, however, counts years with a value of one. If the list is read making the changes, the King List and the Bible tell a similar story. Even if you do not make any changes, the Sumerian King List shows lifespans before the flood were long, and then grew shorter. Also*

the eight kings in the list represent eight generations. The Bible has ten. If you remove Adam and Noah, you have eight. These eight generations may represent the history after Adam until the flood. pg 26

Chapter 3 General Questions

1. Noah's father's name was Lamech, but he was not the same as Lamech who had two wives and was Cain's grandson. Why might Noah's father have given him a name that means rest? *When Noah was born, his father was happy that a son had been added to the family. A son could help keep sheep and goats. He could plant and harvest crops. Farming was hard work, and sons were a blessing. Some think Lamech was remembering the promise of a Deliverer made to Eve to save them from the curse put on them. Lamech saw in Noah this comfort and rest. Noah's father did not have any authority over Satan. He lived thousands of years before Jesus, the promised Deliverer. Striving under Satan's rule, he longed for salvation and rest. pg 29 and 31*

2. Who was Enoch and what happened to him? *Enoch was Noah's great-grandfather. It was said of Enoch that he walked with God. Enoch loved God deeply, and he thought about Him and prayed to Him throughout the day. God was so pleased with Enoch's faith that Enoch was taken away, and some people saw it. Enoch did not die. He was raptured. Enoch was the first person to be described as a man who walked with God. He was also the first person to be raptured. pg 31-32*

3. What began happening to Noah's family, his sisters, brothers, cousins, nieces and nephews? What did Noah decide to do instead? *As he grew, he saw his brothers, his sisters and his cousins turn away from God. They became wicked like their other cousins from Cain's family, and Adam's other sons and daughters. Noah was grieved at the bad things people*

were doing. Noah decided to be like his great-grandfather Enoch and honor God. pg 32

4. How does Genesis 6:9 describe Noah? *It says, "Noah was a just man and perfect in his generations, and Noah walked with God." pg 32*

5. What does it mean that Noah was "perfect in his generations?" *Noah did his best to do what pleased God because he feared, respected and honored, God. He believed God would do what He said He would do. pg 33*

6. How old was Noah when his first son was born? *When Noah was 500 years old, his first son Japheth was born. pg 33*

7. What did God tell Noah to do? *God wanted Noah to build a ship in a specific shape. pg 33*

8. What is a cubit? *A cubit was used in Noah's day instead of feet or meters. It is defined as the distance from a man's elbow to the tip of his middle finger. Recorded distances vary from the shortest, 17.5 inches, to the longest, 20.6 inches. pg 34*

9. How big was the ship Noah built? *We can calculate Noah was to build a ship anywhere from 450 to 510 feet long. According to ArkEncounter. com, 510 feet is one and a half football fields long. The ship was forty to fifty foot high and had three decks contained inside. It was seventy-five to eighty-six feet wide. pg 34*

10. What does têbâh mean and how is it used in Noah's story? *Têbâh means box. The word was used to communicate what type of shape the ship*

would have. We interpret it as ark, which can also mean a chest or box.
The image the word gives us says Noah was supposed to build a cargo ship.
pg 35

11. Is there any evidence in history and archaeology of large ships similar to the size of the ark? If yes, describe one. *Yes, there is evidence of large ships similar in size to the ark. Pliny the Elder gives a list of ancient warships in "Chapter 7" of his Natural History. One of the ships on his list was described by Archbishop James Ussher in his book, Annals of the World. On page 354 he writes: "These types of ships were called Aphracta, but the largest ship of all had eight tiers of oars and was called Leontifera. Others included the Wyoming, and a ship similar to the ark built by Ptolemy Philopater. pg 35-36*

12. Could Noah have used metal in the building of the ark? Why or why not? *Metals were being used before the flood. Tubalcain was "an instructor of every artificer in brass and iron." (Genesis 4:22) Noah could have used metal in his construction, but there is no list of tools, crew or materials. pg 36*

13. What substance did God tell Noah to use to coat the ark? *God instructed Noah to coat the ark with pitch inside and out. pg 36*

14. What is this substance and why was it used? *It could mean a resin. One theory as to why the ark was treated on the inside was to make it impact resistant. pg 37*

15. In Genesis 6:14-16, God says to pitch the ark inside and outside with pitch. But the first pitch is the Hebrew verb *kâphar*. What does

kâphar mean? *It means to cover but also has the meanings to purge, for-give, reconcile, cleanse and atone. pg 37*

16. Did Noah know why he was to build a huge ship called an ark? *No, it was after all the directions that God told Noah why he needed to build an ark. pg 37*

17. How long did it take Noah and his sons to build the ark? *We don't know how long Noah took to build the ark. But within a hundred years it was finished. pg 37*

18. What is surprising about the place Noah built the ark? *He built the ark on dry ground. pg 37*

19. What does it mean to walk by faith? *Walking in faith is operating from a place inside you instead of letting your five senses be your authority. It is giving God's word, the Bible, first place in your life, remaining steady, believing God's words. Nothing else and no one else is placed above it. The final authority is what God has said about a matter instead of what the people or circumstances around you are saying. pg 37-38*

20. What does Genesis 6:22 say about Noah and why do you think it is important? *Noah did all God commanded him to do. Many times God picked people others thought not qualified. But they were diligent to do what was asked of them. Obedience is important to God. pg 38*

21. What does the Bible mean when it says Noah was a preacher of righteousness? *Noah believed, and he was made right with God because of his faith. In both word and actions Noah warned. He was an example of*

what righteousness is. pg 38-39

22. How old was Noah's father Lamech when he died and why might his age be significant? *He was 777 years old. The number seven means completeness and perfection in the Bible. Perhaps it was a sign that the time was near for God to bring the flood. pg 39*

23. Who was Methuselah and what does his name mean? *Methuselah was Noah's grandfather and the man who lived the longest life. His name means man of the dart. pg 39-40*

24. What is important about the year Methuselah died? *He died the year the flood started. pg 40*

25. How many animals might have been on the ark? *There might have been close to 7,000 animals on the ark. pg 40*

26. Why is it important that the ark had only one door? *It was a symbol to illustrate there is only one way to be saved, and that is in believing what God says and trusting Him only. pg 40*

27. After Noah boarded the ark with his wife, his sons and their wives, how long was it until the flooding rains came? *There is some debate on whether Noah entered the ark seven days before the rain started or the day the rain started. pg 41*

28. Who shut the door of the ark? *The Bible says God shut the door of the ark. pg 41*

29. What might those inside the ark have been thinking about as the

rain began? How about those outside the ark? *Answers may vary. pg 41-42*

30. Describe the rain as the Bible defines it. *The Bible says the waters came from above and below. The large piece of land was breaking apart. Water gushed from the openings. The sluice gates in heaven were opened. A sluice is a sliding gate. 'Arubbah (air-roo-BAH) is translated window. It also has these meanings: lattice, chimney and sluice. A sluice holds back a large reserve of water. We use them today to control water near a dam. The gates were opened and a swarming, frothy tide poured out. It was a rainstorm like no other. pg 42*

31. How many years passed from the creation of Adam to the flood? What year might this be on our timeline called BC or Before Christ? *1,656 years had passed from the creation of Adam to the worst flood ever to come upon the earth, a world-wide flood. AM 1656 is also the year 2348 BC. pg 42*

32. What promise did God give Noah after he left the ark? *God made a promise to Noah after he left the ark. God said He would never destroy the earth with a world-wide flood again. To seal His promise, He created a rainbow that appeared in the sky. pg42-43*

33. According to Ezekiel 1:28 and Revelation 4:3, where else can this symbol of the promise be found? *The rainbow is also described as a vision of God's glory, and God's throne has a rainbow around it. pg 43*

Chapter 3 Test Answers

1. How does Genesis 6:9 describe Noah? *It says, "Noah was a just man and perfect in his generations, and Noah walked with God." pg 32*

2. What does it mean that Noah was "perfect in his generations?" *Noah did his best to do what pleased God because he feared, respected and honored, God. He believed God would do what He said He would do. pg 33*

3. What is a cubit? *A cubit was used in Noah's day instead of feet or meters. It is defined as the distance from a man's elbow to the tip of his middle finger. Recorded distances vary from the shortest, 17.5 inches, to the longest, 20.6 inches. pg 34*

4. Describe the rain as the Bible defines it. *The Bible says the waters came from above and below. The large piece of land was breaking apart. Water gushed from the openings. The sluice gates in heaven were opened. A sluice is a sliding gate. 'Arubbah (air-roo-BAH) is translated window. It also has these meanings: lattice, chimney and sluice. A sluice holds back a large reserve of water. We use them today to control water near a dam. The gates were opened and a swarming, frothy tide poured out. It was a rainstorm like no other. pg 42*

5. How many years passed from the creation of Adam to the flood? What year might this be on our timeline called BC or Before Christ? *1,656 years had passed from the creation of Adam to the worst flood ever to come upon the earth, a world-wide flood. AM 1656 is also the year 2348 BC. pg 42*

6. What promise did God give Noah after he left the ark? According to Ezekiel 1:28 and Revelation 4:3, where else can this symbol of the promise be found? *God made a promise to Noah after he left the ark. God said He would never destroy the earth with a world-wide flood again. To seal His promise, He created a rainbow that appeared in the sky. The rainbow is also described as a vision of God's glory, and God's throne has a rainbow around it. pg 42-43*

7. Is there any evidence in history and archaeology of large ships similar to the size of the ark? If yes, describe one. *Yes, there is evidence of large ships similar in size to the ark. Pliny the Elder gives a list of ancient warships in "Chapter 7" of his Natural History. One of the ships on his list was described by Archbishop James Ussher in his book, Annals of the World. On page 354 he writes: "These types of ships were called Aphracta, but the largest ship of all had eight tiers of oars and was called Leontifera. Others included the Wyoming, and a ship similar to the ark built by Ptolemy Philopater. pg 35-36*

8. Could Noah have used metal in the building of the ark? Why or why not? *Metals were being used before the flood. Tubalcain was "an instructor of every artificer in brass and iron." (Genesis 4:22) Noah could have used metal in his construction, but there is no list of tools, crew or materials. pg 36*

9. What does Genesis 6:22 say about Noah and why do you think it is important? *Noah did all God commanded him to do. Many times God picked people others thought not qualified. But they were diligent to do what was asked of them. Obedience is important to God. pg 38*

10. In Genesis 6:14-16, God says to pitch the ark inside and outside with pitch. But the first pitch is the Hebrew verb *kâphar*. What does *kâphar* mean? *It means to cover but also has the meanings to purge, forgive, reconcile, cleanse and atone. pg 37*

Chapter 4 General Questions Answers

1. If Genesis 7:11 tells us when the flood began, why are we not sure when it started? *The Jews use two calendars. Civil and sacred. Some Christian scholars today side with the civil calendar and others with the sacred calendar. pg 45*

2. How many days and nights did it rain? *Forty days and nights the rain continued until the earth was covered with water, even the highest points by more than twenty feet. pg 45-46*

3. What kind of rain was this and how do we know? *The text makes sure we understand it was a continual downpour for at least forty days and nights. This was sheets of blinding rain meeting fountains spewing up from below. The land was breaking apart, causing earthquakes, tsunamis and mudslides. pg46*

4. According to Genesis 7:23 what happened to the people and things of the earth outside the ark? *Genesis 7:23 says, "And every living substance was destroyed which was upon the face of the ground, both man, and cattle, and the creeping things, and the fowl of the heaven; and they were destroyed from the earth: and Noah only remained alive, and they that were with him in the ark." pg 46*

5. How long did it take before the ark began to float? *The Bible says after forty days the ark lifted. pg 46*

6. How many days did it rain all together– in total? *It rained 150 days total. pg 46*

7. What happened after the rain stopped? *After the water flows stopped, the ocean level began to go down until the ark went aground on top of a mountain. in the mountains of Ararat. pg 46*

8. Where did the ark go aground? *The ark went aground in the mountains of Urartu. We say Ararat. Urartu was a region we refer to today as the Armenian Highlands. It includes eastern Turkey, Armenia, Azerbaijan, southern Georgia and northwest Iran. pg 46*

9. What do we know about the land of Ararat? *The land of Urartu or Ararat later became a civilization. It is mentioned in 2Kings 19:36. When the Assyrian King Sennacherib was murdered, his killers escaped to the land of Ararat. Assyria was often in skirmishes with the rulers of Urartu, defeating them only to see them melt into the mountains of their land to rise and fight again. The people are thought to be related to the Hurrians. Ararat was also one of the allied countries to defeat Babylon mentioned in Jeremiah 51:27. pg 47-48*

10. Noah's ark has never been found. Where might it be located? *Mt. Ararat is traditionally the mountain identified with Noah and the ark. Other locations considered are Mt. Cudi in eastern Turkey and Mt. Suleiman in Iran. pg 47*

11. What method did Noah use to see if the water was receding? *Noah sent out birds. He sent out a raven but it came back because it didn't have anywhere to land. He sent out another bird until it did not return. pg 48*

12. How long were Noah and his family on the ark? *He and his family had spent a total of 370 days on the ark. 377 if you include the week before*

God shut the door. pg 48

13. What process did Noah use to free the animals? *He was careful to release them by their groups as God commanded. pg 48*

14. What was the land like outside the ark? *Some trees and plants survived since Noah's dove found an olive leaf. Dead stuff was everywhere. The earth's landscape was drastically changed. There were new mountains, new plants pushing up through the dirt, swampy areas, young trees and tough ones recovering where they still stood. The weather was still affected by volcanoes and warm oceans. It would be a while before everything settled down and the earth was green again. There may have been lingering earth tremors and quakes as the land repositioned itself. pg 48-49*

15. What is the Cradle of Civilization and why is it called that? *The area of the Tigris and Euphrates Rivers is called the Cradle of Civilization. Traditionally experts believed man first began to settle in this region. pg 49*

16. What is the Out of Africa theory? *Evolutionists insist an ape turned into a man near East Africa. They think this early man traveled from Africa to the land of the two rivers. This is called the Out of Africa Theory. pg 49*

17. What are some problems with the Out of Africa theory? *The problem is, these early ape men are not old enough for their timeline. Archaeologists have found towns with the bones of ancient people, their homes, and tools that date to the time this imaginary man-ape is thought to have started his trip. This poses a problem for evolutionists: the African first man was not the first man. Similar towns and their remains are spread over six*

sites in Europe and Asia. The discovery of these towns has made the evolutionists' Out of Africa Theory impossible. pg 49-50

18. What ancient site interests scholars who believe the Bible and why? *For those who believe the Bible, the Dmanisi site is interesting. Dmanisi is about 124 miles north of Mt. Ararat. The fact that groups of people with tools and knowledge who lived in various places throughout the Fertile Crescent at the same time points to what the Bible has said all along: Noah's family moved from the mountains of Ararat and spread out from there. pg 50-51*

19. What is the first thing Noah did when he left the ark? *The first thing Noah did was to worship. He built an altar and made offerings to God. pg 51*

20. What did God tell Noah about the animals? *God told Noah animals would be afraid of him. pg 51*

21. What are the new rules God gave Noah? *The first was permission to eat meat. The second was a law. If an animal or a man killed a person, then that animal or person should die also. pg 52*

22. What command was missing? *God had told Adam to subdue the earth. He did not give this command to Noah. The ability to subdue the earth was lost until Jesus came. pg 52*

23. Did Noah and his sons have to learn to use tools? *No they did not have to learn to use tools. These men had been craftsmen. They built a ship! pg 52*

24. Why were their first homes so primitive? *The world outside the ark was harsh compared to the mild climate before the flood. There were no mature forests for wood to make homes or fires. As Noah's family multiplied, they moved farther from the ark. Shelter became rock outcroppings, caves and reed huts. Tools were made from stones and whatever they salvaged from the ark. pg 52*

25. Noah was six hundred years old when the flood started. How many more years did he live after the flood? *Noah lived another 350 years after the flood. pg 53*

26. What work did Noah do after he left the ark? *He farmed and grew grapes. pg 53*

27. Why did Noah curse Ham's son Canaan? *We may not know for sure, but it has something to do with Noah getting drunk and falling asleep naked in his tent. pg 53*

28. What else do we know about Canaan? *Canaan would become the father of the Canaanites. His name means lowland. They lived in the area of modern day Israel, and Syria. The Ebla Tablets and the Mari Letters reveal much about the culture. They were skilled mathematicians, shipbuilders and sailors. They had rich cities but a wicked culture. Shem and Japheth's children would conquer them later in history. The Canaanites' rule would then be limited to what is today Lebanon. pg 54*

29. Who is Eber and why did he name his son Peleg? *Eber was Shem's great grandson. He named his son Peleg which means divide because the people were divided when God separated them by languages when he was*

born. pg 54-57

30. How did the people who gathered on the plains of Shinar disobey God? *They did not want to travel the earth anymore and they wanted to make a name for themselves instead of honoring God. They wanted to become their own authority. "And they said, Go to, let us build us a city and a tower, whose top may reach unto heaven; and let us make us a name, lest we be scattered abroad upon the face of the whole earth." (Genesis 11:4) pg 55-56*

31. How did the people know how to make bricks and how was their method different than people who lived later? *According to Sanchunia-thon, people had made bricks before the flood. But people in Shinar made bricks by baking them in a kiln. Israelites and those living in the Promised Land made sun dried bricks and mud for mortar. The people in Shinar used tar similar to asphalt as mortar. The result was walls stronger than rock. pg 56*

32. What does this method of brick-making tell us about the building they were constructing? *This type of construction was expensive and took time. It was reserved for important buildings like palaces and temples. What the Bible is telling us is this building was important and expensive. pg 56*

33. What is the traditional name for this building? *It is called the Tower of Babel (baw-BEL), and it means the tower of confusion. pg 56*

34. What do we think this structure looked like? *The Tower of Babel probably was a ziggurat or resembled one. pg 56*

35. What was God's response to the people's building project? *God came down and saw the people's tower and the desire of their hearts. He knew if they continued in their unity, the world would become evil quickly, the same as in the days before the flood. "And the LORD said, Behold, the people is one, and they have all one language; and this they begin to do: and now nothing will be restrained from them, which they have imagined to do." (Genesis 11:6) pg 57*

36. Is there any archaeological evidence pointing to the beginning of different languages? *This happened during the time Peleg lived. It so stunned Eber, he named his son Division. This is also why different languages such as Greek and Egyptian are dated to the time shortly after Peleg was born. pg 57 and 54-55*

37. What does the account of the Tower of Babel explain? *The Tower of Babel explains why people speak different languages. pg 57-58*

38. How many language roots are there and where did many of them begin? *Some think there are twenty different families while others say seventy-eight. All counts seem to be under 100. Modern evolutionists are beginning to agree many language roots had their start near the country of Turkey. pg 58*

For Further Study: What might different languages with shared sounds and meanings indicate? *They share an original source.* Why do you think questions about man's unique ability to speak are troublesome? *Answers will vary,*

39. What does people speaking similar languages tell us about them?

Today we know people with similar languages are related to each other. This means God probably kept children and parents together. pg 58

Activity: Compare greetings like hello or the words for goodbye in French, Italian, Portuguese, English, German and Spanish. You can use an online translation service if you are able to access the internet. Listen to their pronunciations. Write them down. Now find the same greetings in Chinese. Do they sound similar? Using the same languages, find the word for water. Continue to compare languages. Are there any you think might be related? *All of them are Indo-European languages except Chinese.*

Activity: Read pages 58-59 again. Explain how the human genome and the study of DNA support the account of Genesis and the Table of Nations in Genesis 10. *Researchers who study DNA have discovered "the human genome began to rapidly diversify about 5,000 years ago." The diversity came because at first it was just Noah's sons having kids. Then it multiplied, and multiplied as their families grew up and continued to have children. The Table of Nations shows us who some of them were and what countries came from them.*

40. Why is unity called a tool? *Unity can be used to accomplish a good thing or a bad thing. It is a tool men use to accomplish good and evil. pg 59*

Chapter 4 Test 1 Answers

1. If Genesis 7:11 tells us when the flood began, why are we not sure when it started? *The Jews use two calendars. Civil and sacred. Some Christian scholars today side with the civil calendar and others with the sacred calendar. pg 45*

2. How many days and nights did it rain? *Forty days and nights the rain continued until the earth was covered with water, even the highest points by more than twenty feet. pg 45-46*

3. According to Genesis 7:23 what happened to the people and things of the earth outside the ark? *Genesis 7:23 says, "And every living substance was destroyed which was upon the face of the ground, both man, and cattle, and the creeping things, and the fowl of the heaven; and they were destroyed from the earth: and Noah only remained alive, and they that were with him in the ark." pg 46*

4. How many days did it rain all together– in total? *It rained 150 days total. pg 46*

5. How long were Noah and his family on the ark? *He and his family had spent a total of 370 days on the ark. 377 if you include the week before God shut the door. pg 48*

6. What was the land like outside the ark? *Some trees and plants survived since Noah's dove found an olive leaf. Dead stuff was everywhere. The earth's landscape was drastically changed. There were new mountains, new plants pushing up through the dirt, swampy areas, young trees and tough*

ones recovering where they still stood. The weather was still affected by volcanoes and warm oceans. It would be a while before everything settled down and the earth was green again. There may have been lingering earth tremors and quakes as the land repositioned itself. pg 48-49

7. What is the Out of Africa theory and what are some problems with this theory? *Evolutionists insist an ape turned into a man near East Africa. They think this early man traveled from Africa to the land of the two rivers. This is called the Out of Africa Theory. The problem is, these early ape men are not old enough for the evolutionists' timeline. Archaeologists have found towns with the bones of ancient people, their homes, and tools that date to the time this imaginary man-ape is thought to have started his trip. This poses a problem for evolutionists: the African first man was not the first man. Similar towns and their remains are spread over six sites in Europe and Asia. The discovery of these towns has made the evolutionists' Out of Africa Theory impossible. pg 49-50*

8. When God gave Noah His new rules what command was missing and why? *God had told Adam to subdue the earth. He did not give this command to Noah. The ability to subdue the earth was lost until Jesus came. pg 52*

9. What ancient site interests scholars who believe the Bible and why? *For those who believe the Bible, the Dmanisi site is interesting. Dmanisi is about 124 miles north of Mt. Ararat. The fact that groups of people with tools and knowledge who lived in various places throughout the Fertile Crescent at the same time points to what the Bible has said all along: Noah's family moved from the mountains of Ararat and spread out from there. pg 50-51*

10. What is the first thing Noah did when he left the ark? *The first thing Noah did was to worship. He built an altar and made offerings to God. pg 51*

Chapter 4 Test 2 Answers

1. Did Noah and his sons have to learn to use tools? *No they did not have to learn to use tools. These men had been craftsmen. They built a ship! pg 52*

2. Why were their first homes so primitive? *The world outside the ark was harsh compared to the mild climate before the flood. There were no mature forests for wood to make homes or fires. As Noah's family multiplied, they moved farther from the ark. Shelter became rock outcroppings, caves and reed huts. Tools were made from stones and whatever they salvaged from the ark. pg 52*

3. What else do we know about Canaan other than Noah cursed him? *Canaan would become the father of the Canaanites. His name means lowland. They lived in the area of modern day Israel, and Syria. The Ebla Tablets and the Mari Letters reveal much about the culture. They were skilled mathematicians, shipbuilders and sailors. They had rich cities but a wicked culture. Shem and Japheth's children would conquer them later in history. The Canaanites' rule would then be limited to what is today Lebanon. pg 54*

4. Who is Eber and why did he name his son Peleg? *Eber was Shem's*

great grandson and he named his son Peleg which means divide because the people were divided when God separated them by languages when he was born. pg 54-57

5. How did the people know how to make bricks and how was their method different than people who lived later? What does this method of brick-making tell us about the building they were constructing? *According to Sanchuniathon, people had made bricks before the flood. But people in Shinar made bricks by baking them in a kiln. Israelites and those living in the Promised Land made sun dried bricks and mud for mortar. The people in Shinar used tar similar to asphalt as mortar. The result was walls stronger than rock. This type of construction was expensive and took time. It was reserved for important buildings like palaces and temples. What the Bible is telling us is this building was important and expensive. pg 56*

6. Why did the people of Shinar build a tower and what do we think this structure looked like? *They did not want to travel the earth anymore and they wanted to make a name for themselves instead of honoring God. They wanted to become their own authority. "And they said, Go to, let us build us a city and a tower, whose top may reach unto heaven; and let us make us a name, lest we be scattered abroad upon the face of the whole earth." (Genesis 11:4) The Tower of Babel probably was a ziggurat or resembled one. pg 55-56*

7. Is there any archaeological evidence pointing to the beginning of different languages? *This happened during the time Peleg lived. It so stunned Eber, he named his son Division. This is also why different languages such as Greek and Egyptian are dated to the time shortly after Peleg was born.*

pg 57 and 54-55

8. What does the account of the Tower of Babel explain? *The Tower of Babel explains why people speak different languages. pg 57-58*

9. How many language roots are there and where did many of them begin? *Some think there are twenty different families while others say seventy-eight. All counts seem to be under 100. Modern evolutionists are beginning to agree many language roots had their start near the country of Turkey. pg 58*

10. What does people speaking similar languages tell us about them? *Today we know people with similar languages are related to each other. This means God probably kept children and parents together. pg 58*

Chapter 5 General Questions

1. Who is George Smith and what is one of his achievements? *George Smith was born in England in 1840. He had to go to work when he was fourteen, but he educated himself and indulged in his passion for Assyrian culture. Among his achievements is the translation of an Assyrian legend found on tablets in the Royal Library of Ashurbanipal. Smith discovered a "mutilated account" of what he said was the Tower of Babel. pg 61*

2. Is there any other ancient literature besides the Bible that tells the story of the Tower of Babel? If so, name one. *Yes, the Assyrian account is not the only story related to the Tower of Babel. It is also told in the Sumerian myth, Enmerkar and the lord of Aratta. pg 62-63*

3. Where can Tower and language legends be found? *Tower and language legends can be found scattered throughout the earth. For example, Mexico, Nepal, Africa, Australia and Arizona have such legends. pg 62-63*

4. What is a myth? *A myth is thought to be a made up story and uses symbols to teach an idea or moral. pg 64*

5. What is an etiological myth? *Etiological myths are myths trying to explain creation or some other aspect of life not understood. pg 64*

6. What is a legend? *A legend is a story that has some truth to it and can be based on a real person or group. pg 64*

7. How do we decide what is a myth and what is a legend? *We decide*

what is myth and what is legend sometimes by observation, and it can also depend on what we believe to be true. pg 64-65

8. Where can flood myths be found? *Flood myths be found all over the world on all continents.* pg 65

9. What do you think is important about flood myths? *Answers will vary.*

10. Describe the two versions of the Babylonian story called the *Atrahasis Epic. One version says the flood was caused by too many people on the earth. One of the gods was annoyed by the noise, and the other gods decided to destroy all the people. One god, Enki, warned a man named Atrahasis who built a boat with plans given him by the god. In another version, Enki warned a king named Ziusudra. The king built a boat that Enki described to him, and he floated on the floodwaters for seven days. The king opened a window in the boat and offered sacrifices to a sky god. Those who believe the Genesis Flood is a myth think Noah was really Ziusudra.* pg 67

11. What is the most famous Babylonian flood story? *The most famous Babylonian flood story is the Epic of Gilgamesh.* pg 67

12. Who was Hormuzd Rassam? *Hormuzd Rassam was an Assyrian Christian archaeologist.* pg 67-68

13. Tell about Rassam's discovery. *In 1853 Rassam discovered a complete set of worn and broken tablets when he excavated King Ashurbanipal's library at Ninevah. Rassam did not know the importance of his discovery because parts of the tablets weren't translated until nineteen years later. The*

tablets were The Epic of Gilgamesh. pg 67-68

14. Who translated the tablets known as the *Epic of Gilgamesh*? *George Smith was the man who translated them. pg 68*

15. Are the *Atrahasis Epic* and the *Epic of Gilgamesh* original stories? *No, they are copies. Some scholars think the Atrahasis Epic may have been the source for Gilgamesh's flood story. Other experts believe Gilgamesh's Epic came first. Both seem to be copies of another source, only no one knows what it is. Christians believe they know the source: Noah's life story told in Genesis. pg 68*

16. Who was Gilgamesh and what did he do? *He was a real king of Uruk and the main character in he Epic of Gilgamesh. He lived after the flood, perhaps around 2700 BC. The Epic begins by describing him as wise and knowledgeable about the countries around him, the secret things, in essence all things. He went on a long journey and brought the people back a story about the days before the flood. He wrote the story on stone tablets. pg 68*

17. In your own words tell the story of the *Epic of Gilgamesh. Answers will vary. pg 68-69*

18. Why does Nozomi Osanai believe the Genesis account of the flood is the original account? *She points out that 95% of the flood stories told around the world have common elements to the Genesis account. Not the Epic of Gilgamesh. pg 69*

19. Who are the Miao people and why is their flood story amazing?

The Miao people live in China. Their method of recording a story repeats itself. The second sentence explains the first by saying it in a different way similar to the Hebrew method. Their flood story is the closest to the Genesis account of the flood. pg70-71

20. What are geological evidences for the flood? *Scientists recently discovered crystallized ice about 500 miles below the earth's surface. The study shows pockets of water are also possible that deep. If you cut into the earth exposing rock layers in various parts of the earth, thick layers of mud and sand are mixed with fossils and animal skeletons. Rock from the Appalachians can be found in the desert southwest, and sea life is found buried on top of mountains. In the Grand Canyon bent rock layers can be seen, forming the same shape top to bottom as if they were laid down quickly and sagged. pg 71*

21. How are fossils formed? *Most people think fossils form over long periods of time. Actually they form quickly if buried and out of reach...like in flood conditions. pg 71*

22. How do jellyfish point to a worldwide flood? *Jellyfish are soft creatures that float when dead or turn to goo if beached. Scientists say the fossils of jellyfish were formed within hours from a terrible tropical storm. These fossils are found in various unlikely places like Australia, Utah, Death Valley and in Wisconsin under twelve feet of rock. The "storm" was obviously a violent worldwide event that fossilized alot of jellyfish instantly. pg 72*

23. Describe the K-T event. *The K-T event is a world-wide mass extinction of 75% of plant and animal life on the earth. Evolutionists say it happened 66 million years ago and was caused by a comet and volcanoes.*

The event is recorded in a thin layer of sediment called the K-G boundary. pg 72-73

24. Compare the evolutionists' view of the geologic column with Dr. Andrew Snelling's view. *Evolutionists say the layers are separated by millions of years. There are several theories to interpret the column. In one theory there are twelve layers. This is supposedly the proof of evolution from smaller creatures to larger. Any observed fossils that don't fit their assigned time period are called misplaced fossils. Dr. Andrew Snelling says the layers are caused by the flood, and they are where they are to be expected. First the waters of the deep were broken causing surging waters which buried sea life quickly. As the waters rose, fish then land animals and plants were killed. They are found in the upper layers of rock where you imagine they would be. pg 73*

25. Could any of the layers of the geological column have happened slowly? *None of these layers could have happened slowly. Creatures could have escaped death if they had time to run or swim for it. Instead, mass graves are found. pg 73*

26. What did Darwin realize? *Darwin realized the flaw in his theory was magnified by the fossil record. pg 73*

27. Who was Melchizedek and why is he important to our study? *There are many lessons to learn from this man. Ours in this study is he was worshipping God before the Israelites were born, at the same time as Abraham and after Noah's flood— in the land of Eber. The true message was being kept by some people. pg 74*

Activity: Read Ephesians 4:17-18, and then write it your own words. *Answers will vary. pg 74*

28. What does *mataiotēs* mean? *The Greek word translated vanity is mataiotēs (mah-tie-AH- taze). It means without truth, perverse, weak. pg 74*

29. What is our understanding like when we separate from God? *Our understanding is without truth, perverse and weak when we separate from God and His word. pg 74*

30. What lesson can we learn from the Miao people? *The Miao people, who so carefully saved their story of creation and Noah, took the false gods of their neighbors as their own. The lesson is we choose what we believe and who we follow. We must make a decision to read the Bible and follow everything God tells us to do. pg 74-75*

Chapter 5 Test Answers

1. Is there any other ancient literature besides the Bible that tells the story of the Tower of Babel? If so, name one. *Yes, the Assyrian account is not the only story related to the Tower of Babel. It is also told in the Sumerian myth, Enmerkar and the lord of Aratta. pg 62-63*

2. Where can Tower, flood and language legends be found? *Tower, flood and language legends can be found all around the world. pg 63-65*

3. What is an etiological myth? *Etiological myths are myths trying to explain creation or some other aspect of life not understood. pg 64*

4. Are the *Atrahasis Epic* and the *Epic of Gilgamesh* original stories? *No, they are copies. Some scholars think the Atrahasis Epic may have been the source for Gilgamesh's flood story. Other experts believe Gilgamesh's Epic came first. Both seem to be copies of another source, only no one knows what it is. Christians believe they know the source: Noah's life story told in Genesis. pg 68*

5. Why does Nozomi Osanai believe the Genesis account of the flood is the original account? *She points out that 95% of the flood stories told around the world have common elements to the Genesis account. Not the Epic of Gilgamesh. pg 69*

6. How do jellyfish point to a worldwide flood? *Jellyfish are soft creatures that float when dead or turn to goo if beached. Scientists say the fossils of jellyfish were formed within hours from a terrible tropical storm. These fossils are found in various unlikely places like Australia, Utah, Death Valley*

and in Wisconsin under twelve feet of rock. The "storm" was obviously a violent worldwide event that fossilized alot of jellyfish instantly. pg 72

7. Compare the evolutionists' view of the geologic column with Dr. Andrew Snelling's view. *Evolutionists say the layers are separated by millions of years. There are several theories to interpret the column. In one theory there are twelve layers. This is supposedly the proof of evolution from smaller creatures to larger. Any observed fossils that don't fit their assigned time period are called misplaced fossils. Dr. Andrew Snelling says the layers are caused by the flood, and they are where they are to be expected. First the waters of the deep were broken causing surging waters which buried sea life quickly. As the waters rose, fish then land animals and plants were killed. They are found in the upper layers of rock where you imagine they would be. pg 73*

8. Could any of the layers of the geological column have happened slowly? *None of these layers could have happened slowly. Creatures could have escaped death if they had time to run or swim for it. Instead, mass graves are found. pg 73*

9. What did Darwin realize? *Darwin realized the flaw in his theory was magnified by the fossil record. pg 73*

10. Who was Melchizedek and why is he important to our study? *There are many lessons to learn from this man. Ours in this study is he was worshipping God before the Israelites were born, at the same time as Abraham and after Noah's flood— in the land of Eber. The true message was being kept by some people. pg 74*

Chapter 6 General Questions

1. Name some ziggurats you can visit in the Middle East and tell where they are located. *The Dūr Untash ziggurat in Iran, Tepe Sialk in Kāshān, Iran, The Great Ziggurat of Ur is in the Dhi Qar Province of Iraq, the Tongue Tower in Borsippa, Iraq, Etemenanki in Iraq, pg 77-80*

2. How long does it take to walk around the foundation of the Great Ziggurat in Iraq? *An American soldier walked around the base of the Great Ziggurat in forty-five minutes. pg 77*

3. What were ziggurats used for? *Scholars debate how ancient people used ziggurats. But the ziggurats' names inscribed on ancient clay bricks reveal they were used at least partially for religious temples. The ziggurat in Ur was part of a group of buildings used for government offices and a religious center. pg 78*

4. What is the Enuma Elish and what do some scholars think it shows us about the people living after the flood? *The Enuma Elish is a story about gods building a tower to live in. Some believe these early descendants of Noah were bringing back gods worshipped before the flood. pg 78-79*

5. What might the eight kings listed on the Sumerian King List show us? *The King List may be insight into other sons of Adam and their lines. pg 79*

6. What kind of religion did the people of Babylon develop? *Babylon developed a religious system worshipping the sun, moon and stars, where the number eight is seen repeatedly. pg 79*

For Further Study: Considering this, why should we be careful of the types of games we play, books we read and shows or movies we watch? What can you do to protect yourself from these influences or when you are pressured to join in with your friends? *Answers will vary.*

7. What word did Moses use to describe a ziggurat and why? *Moses used the word migdol (mig-DOLL) which means tower to describe the building Noah's descendants built. Migdol has the meaning of a pyramid shape and can be used for a strong, fortified place. This may give us another image of what Moses wanted to communicate. pg 80*

8. What do ziggurats reveal about the desire of the people who built them? *A ziggurat is an image of an ancient, unbelieving man's desperation and longing for a god who loved him and would help him. pg 80-81*

9. How is the God of the Bible different than the false gods the people worshipped? *The God of the Bible walked with Adam. His presence was known by Enoch. He spoke to Cain. He spoke to Noah. He would travel with the Israelites in the desert. He would dwell in the Tabernacle and the Temple. He would be called Emmanuel, God With Us. John would write, "... the Word was God...And the Word was made flesh, and dwelt among us." (John 1:1 and 14.) pg 81*

10. Why couldn't the Tower of Babel be the ziggurat Nebuchadnez-zar I or Nebuchadnezzar II built? *The Tower of Babel was built around a hundred years after the flood. Dates range from 2250-2242BC. But Nebuchadnezzar I reigned during the Middle Babylonian period. He built a temple in Nippur for the god Enlil around 1124-1104 BC. Dr. Andrew George from the University of London says Nebuchadnezzar's ziggurat in-*

spired the Bible's Tower of Babel story. That's impossible. He says that be-
cause the Jews were captives in Babylon under Nebuchadnezzar II. But the
Jews were captives in 605 BC. Neither Nebuchadnezzar could have built
the original tower because they lived hundreds of years later. pg 81

11. Does the Bible actually say Tower of Babel? *The Bible never calls the*
tower, the Tower of Babel. pg 81

12. How many ziggurats do we know of in Mesopotamia? *There are*
a total of twenty-nine ziggurats we know of in Mesopotamia and ancient
literature. pg 81

Activity: Compare the step pyramids of Mesoamerica with the ziggurats in the Middle East. The biggest step pyramid is the Great Pyramid
of Cholula in Puebla Mexico. The Pyramid of Kukulkan is a Mayan
Temple. There are six step pyramids in Yalbac, Belize. Perhaps the most
famous Mesoamerican ziggurat is an Aztec temple, the Pyramid of the
Sun. Find a picture of it. What was it used for? Why are these Mesoamerican structures called step pyramids and the others ziggurats? *The*
Mesoamerican ziggurats were used for religious purposes. The Mesoamer-
ican "step pyramids" are ziggurats. Their construction is a bit different,
however. Rubble is piled up and bricks overlay it.

13. Who are the Halaf people? *A culture supposedly dating to 6,000 BC*
is the Halaf (HAL-uf) people. They seem to have migrated south out of the
Armenian Highlands into Turkey, Syria and Iraq. They raised cattle, sheep,
goats and knew how to adapt farming methods to the dry climate. They
grew wheat, barley and flax. pg 82

14. Who are the Ubaid people and what was their culture like? *Some scholars date the invention of the ziggurat to the time of the Ubaid (oo-BADE) people, a group that came after the Halaf people. Both cultures built round or rectangular mud-brick homes with multiple rooms. Their homes were constructed on stone foundations, and their villages were unwalled, suggesting peaceful relations with others. There were craftsmen who worked with metal. There were weavers and pottery makers who made various forms of pottery. They painted and decorated with geometric designs or drawings of animals. The craftsmen made these products for home use and trade. The Halaf and Ubaid cultures are thought to be older than the people who developed the cities of Shinar into an empire. pg 82*

15. When did civilization begin? *Civilization actually began in Eden and east of it. pg 83*

16. Where did civilization begin after the flood? *The traditional view is civilization started in southern Iraq and spread north. This opinion is influenced by Genesis 10:10 describing Nimrod's territory, but it fails to consider earlier people like Noah and his sons. Recent discoveries indicate civilization began near the Caucasus Mountains and spread south. This would explain the Halaf and Ubaid people and their villages, the people living before Nimrod built his cities. pg 83*

17. What does *bâlal* mean? *Bâlal is the Hebrew word used for confused. pg 83*

18. What does the Bible reveal about the Shinar? *We know from the Bible Shinar was an array of settlements which became Babylon, the empire. pg 84*

19. Who were the Sumerians? *There are two stories of how the people came into Sumer, especially into the ancient cities of southern Iraq. Both could be correct. One story is of a people who call themselves the black headed people. They say they came from the north, an area we identify today with the Caucasus Mountain Range which includes the Armenian Highlands. Another is they came from the east and joined Semites who were already settling in the plains. The people living there became who we know as Sumerians. pg 84-85*

20. What do we know about the Sumerian language? *The Sumerian language is not related to any ancient languages of its day. It also does not appear that any new people arrived in the Ubaid or Halaf settlements speaking this language. There is no proof of different pottery styles, and their myths are the same as the rest of the region. Archaeologists conclude from this there is no Sumerian race. People became Sumerian. pg 85*

21. Why is Eridu a good candidate for the city where the Tower of Babel is located? *Sumerian scribes said it was the oldest city in the world. It is thought to date to 5400 BC. Eridu was the source of the first pagan flood story, the Atrahasis Epic. It has a story describing a garden much like the one in Eden. The earliest evidence of sailing boats is found in Eridu and dates to the Ubaid people. It also has a ziggurat dating to the Ubaid culture and before the Sumerian culture. Cuneiform tablets call it Nun-Ki or Mighty Place. Nun-ki is also used for the word Babylon. Berossus, an ancient Babylonian historian, calls Eridu Babylon. The Sumerian King List states it was where "the kingship descended from heaven." Two ancient myths seem to indicate Eridu. Its tower and city were abandoned. Eridu covered about 100 acres and thousands of people lived there. pg 85*

22. Why are ziggurats found all over the earth? *The idea of ziggurats caught on and was taken with people as they traveled from Babel. That is why you find them scattered over the earth. pg 86*

23. What is the Uruk Expansion? *The Uruk Expansion is the dispersal of people after the Tower of Babel. When archaeologists find settlements and cities everywhere at the same time, they are witnessing what is called the dispersal, the scattering of the people after their languages were divided. They label it the Uruk Expansion and assign it a period, the Uruk Period. They place it after the Ubaid Period. In the Uruk Expansion space of time, they list the rise of civilization and the skill of writing. pg 86*

Activity: Draw a picture of the Uruk Expansion. *Answers will vary.*

24. What followed the forced separation at Babel? *Expansion, trade and widespread wealth and civilizations followed the forced separation at Babel. pg 86*

25. Name some settlements that date to this period. *Some settlements included in this period are Hacinebi and Samsat in Turkey, Jebel Aruda, Tell Brak and Habuba Kabira in Syria, Gesher Benot Ya'aqov in Israel (creationists' view), Godin Tepe, Chogha Mish and Susa in Iran. pg 86*

26. What do finds at Çatalhöyük and Ain Ghazal reveal? *Finds in Çatalhöyük Turkey and Ain Ghazal Jordan have shown that farming was part of the ancient world when evolutionists expected people to only know how to hunt and gather food. Evidence of sheep, goats, two kinds of wheat, almonds, peas, lentils and vetch have been found at the site. pg 86*

27. Why did the Ohalo II village surprise the experts? *Ohalo II reveals people were fishing and harvesting grains, vegetables and fruits even though they date this village to 23,000 years ago before they thought man was capable of knowing and doing such things. pg 86*

28. Why does it seem the ancient agricultural revolution burst on the scene in areas of Mesopotamia at the same time? *The agricultural revolution as it is called began in Mesopotamia, and according to genetic research of plants burst on the scene in Turkey, Syria, Iran and Iraq at the same time because it was the people living after the flood, moving out from the mountains near the ark. They knew how to farm because Noah was a farmer. pg 87*

29. Who is Ötzi and what does he show us about the people living near the time of the Tower of Babel incident? *He was the victim of an ancient murder. He was found in the Ötzal Alps. Ötzi was well able to think, plan and provide. He may have been employed as a trader or shepherd. Ötzi had many skills common to modern man and even his problems. pg 88*

30. Why is the list in Genesis 10 called the Table of Nations important? *The list in Genesis 10 is important because it tells us the beginnings of nations and countries. pg 89-90*

Chapter 6 Test Answers

1. What is the *Enuma Elish* and what do some scholars think it shows us about the people living after the flood? *The Enuma Elish is a story about gods building a tower to live in. Some believe these early descendants of Noah were bringing back gods worshipped before the flood. pg 78-79*

2. What word did Moses use to describe a ziggurat and why? *Moses used the word migdol (mig-DOLL) which means tower to describe the building Noah's descendants built. Migdol has the meaning of a pyramid shape and can be used for a strong, fortified place. This may give us another image of what Moses wanted to communicate. pg 80*

3. What do ziggurats reveal about the desire of the people who built them? *A ziggurat is an image of an ancient, unbelieving man's desperation and longing for a god who loved him and would help him. pg 80-81*

4. Why couldn't the Tower of Babel be the ziggurat Nebuchadnezzar I or Nebuchadnezzar II built? *The Tower of Babel was built around a hundred years after the flood. Dates range from 2250-2242BC. But Nebuchadnezzar I reigned during the Middle Babylonian period. He built a temple in Nippur for the god Enlil around 1124-1104 BC. Dr. Andrew George from the University of London says Nebuchadnezzar's ziggurat inspired the Bible's Tower of Babel story. That's impossible. He says that because the Jews were captives in Babylon under Nebuchadnezzar II. But the Jews were captives in 605 BC. Neither Nebuchadnezzar could have built the original tower because they lived hundreds of years later. pg 81*

5. Who were the Sumerians? *There are two stories of how the people came*

into Sumer, especially into the ancient cities of southern Iraq. Both could be correct. One story is of a people who call themselves the black headed people. They say they came from the north, an area we identify today with the Caucasus Mountain Range which includes the Armenian Highlands. Another is they came from the east and joined Semites who were already settling in the plains. The people living there became who we know as Sumerians. pg 84-85

6. What do we know about the Sumerian language? *The Sumerian language is not related to any ancient languages of its day. It also does not appear that any new people arrived in the Ubaid or Halaf settlements speaking this language. There is no proof of different pottery styles, and their myths are the same as the rest of the region. Archaeologists conclude from this there is no Sumerian race. People became Sumerian. pg 85*

7. Why is Eridu a good candidate for the city where the Tower of Babel is located? *Sumerian scribes said it was the oldest city in the world. It is thought to date to 5400 BC. Eridu was the source of the first pagan flood story, the Atrahasis Epic. It has a story describing a garden much like the one in Eden. The earliest evidence of sailing boats is found in Eridu and dates to the Ubaid people. It also has a ziggurat dating to the Ubaid culture and before the Sumerian culture. Cuneiform tablets call it Nun-Ki or Mighty Place. Nun-ki is also used for the word Babylon. Berossus, an ancient Babylonian historian, calls Eridu Babylon. The Sumerian King List states it was where "the kingship descended from heaven." Two ancient myths seem to indicate Eridu. Its tower and city were abandoned. Eridu covered about 100 acres and thousands of people lived there. pg 85*

8. What is the Uruk Expansion? *The Uruk Expansion is the dispersal of*

people after the Tower of Babel. When archaeologists find settlements and cities everywhere at the same time, they are witnessing what is called the dispersal, the scattering of the people after their languages were divided. They label it the Uruk Expansion and assign it a period, the Uruk Period. They place it after the Ubaid Period. In the Uruk Expansion space of time, they list the rise of civilization and the skill of writing. pg 86

9. Why does it seem the ancient agricultural revolution burst on the scene in areas of Mesopotamia at the same time? *The agricultural revolution as it is called began in Mesopotamia, and according to genetic research of plants burst on the scene in Turkey, Syria, Iran and Iraq at the same time because it was the people living after the flood, moving out from the mountains near the ark. They knew how to farm because Noah was a farmer. pg 87*

10. Why is the list in Genesis 10 called the Table of Nations important? *The list in Genesis 10 is important because it tells us the beginnings of nations and countries. pg 89-90*

Chapter 7 General Questions

1. What do we know about the Sumerian King List? *The Sumerian King List was found in Nippur, Iraq in 1906. The most complete version of the List is a stone cube eight inches tall with cuneiform writing on its sides. It is chipped, cracked and worn in spots. It is thought that the hole running through the center of the cube was for a spindle so the cube could be turned and read easily. The List is a type of recorded history, like our Presidents' names and years in office written in a book. pg 93*

2. Why do some say there was a pre-Adamite civilization? *Evolutionists face big challenges with the King List. They date the List to around 266,000 years ago. But they think apes became men around 200,000 years ago and they date the rise of civilization, including kings, to around 6,000 years ago. To solve the problem their dates create, they say there was a pre-Adamite civilization of archaic humans which became extinct. pg 94*

3. What does the Sumerian King List say about a flood? *After the listing of eight kings it says, "Then the flood swept over." pg 95*

4. What did Henry Rawlinson conclude about the Sumerians? *Henry Rawlinson concluded from his research the Semitic and non-Semitic speakers who founded Mesopotamia were both black skinned and called themselves black heads. He considered them Cushites. pg 95*

5. What type of government is described on the Sumerian King List? *We observe from the List a city-state system. pg 95*

6. What did scholars first think about the kings on the Sumerian King

List? *Scholars first thought all the kings were characters in mythical tales. pg 95*

7. Who was the first king to be identified as a real king? *Enmebaragesi is the earliest Cushite king to be confirmed as a real ruler. pg 95*

8. What tower myth is connected to one of the kings on the List and what is the king's name? *Enmerkar is among the kings on the Sumerian King List. He is named as the second king of Uruk and its builder. Enmerkar and the Lord of Aratta tells the story of how Enmerkar wanted to build a temple for the god Enki at Eridu but was stopped because the languages were confused. He prayed for man to speak one language again. He said the god Enki had changed one language into many because of ambitious lords, princes and kings. pg 96*

9. Who is Gilgamesh and what is the name of his flood story? *Gilgamesh was the king of Uruk or Erech as the Bible spells it. (Iraq comes from the word Erech.) He is listed as the fifth king of Uruk on the Sumerian King List. His flood story is called The Epic of Gilgamesh. pg 97*

10. According to his story, what was Gilgamesh like? *Gilgamesh was handsome and strong. No one could beat him. He was lord over men according to the Epic, and he built the walls of Uruk with baked bricks and overlaid the exterior with copper. He went out into the lands around, and the Epic says "no son was left to his father" because he took them all. The women too. Before young girls could marry, they had to act like his wife. The people complained Gilgamesh was not a good king. He did not take care of the people like a shepherd would his sheep. pg 97*

11. Who was Enkidu? *Enkidu was Gilgamesh's enemy. He was a man with long, perhaps brownish blonde hair, and a hairy body. He too was strong and muscular. Though they were enemies at first, after Gilgamesh fought Enkidu, they became friends. Later they went on a journey together. pg 97*

12. Briefly explain what happened in the Forest Journey. *Answer should include any of the following:*

Gilgamesh said his name had not been inscribed on bricks where famous men lived, the Country of the Living. He wanted to go to this great forest because there was an evil god there. Enkidu did not want to go at first and warned Gilgamesh against trying to fight the god who never slept and guarded the forest. They set off, crossing mountains and finally arrived in the forest. It mentions Lebanon, a place in the Bible known for its cedars. Some think the mountain he went to was Mt. Hermon. Gilgamesh used sorcery to give him dreams and guidance. Huwawa, god of the forest, had the face of a lion, and his voice roared like that of a flood. But when this god spoke to him, Gilgamesh fell down as if dead. He killed the god Huwawa. Gilgamesh also killed the god called the Bull of Heaven sent to destroy men and crops. After his friend Enkidu died, Gilgamesh began thinking about his own death. He realized while some people were dying, there were those who lived extremely long. He wanted to live forever. Gilgamesh went to visit his relative Utnapishtim. Utnapishtim was ancient and thought to be immortal. The god Enki had commanded Utnapishtim to build a big ship called the Preserver of Life. On this ship he was to take his family, baby animals and food. Utnapishtim did not like Gilgamesh, but his wife felt sorry for him. He then gave Gilgamesh a plant to make him young. But on the way home a serpent stole the plant, and Gilgamesh gave up the idea of living forever. pg 98-99

13. Who do some scholars think Gilgamesh is in the Bible? *Some scholars and Christian historians think Gilgamesh was really Nimrod. pg 99*

14. What does the Bible say about Nimrod and how does it describe him? *Genesis 10:8-12 gives us a history of Nimrod. "And Cush begat Nimrod: he began to be a mighty one in the earth. He was a mighty hunter before the LORD: wherefore it is said, Even as Nimrod the mighty hunter before the LORD." (Genesis 8:9-10) He was the first powerful man after the flood. The word translated mighty one or powerful is gibbôwr (gib-ORE), and it means valiant, warrior, tyrant and champion. pg 99*

15. What does the word Nimrod mean? *Nimrod translated into Hebrew means rebellious. pg 100*

16. What are the similarities between Nimrod and Gilgamesh? *Both are described as powerful. Both are considered sinful and in opposition to the God who never sleeps and whose voice is like thunder. Nimrod lived during the time of Noah and witnessed younger generations born with shorter life spans. pg 100*

17. What truths are hidden in the *Epic of Gilgamesh? Gilgamesh, an early king wanted to know Utnapishtim's secret for long life. Utnapishtim is a Noah-like figure. Also, in Gilgamesh's story the serpent stole man's ability to live forever on the earth, a story Nimrod would have known about Adam and Eve. Some wonder if the god Huwawa is the YHWH (Yahweh) of the Bible. Mt. Hermon is in the Golan Heights of Israel. The Jordan*

River begins nearby. It was the home of the nephalim, giants, in the Old Testament. King Solomon called it the Tower of Lebanon. It is where Peter proclaimed Jesus the Messiah in Matthew 16:16 among the old high places of Baal. Many think this is where the Transfiguration of Matthew 17 took place. If this is where Gilgamesh went, the location may be significant. pg 100-101

18. What was Gilgamesh's purpose for writing the *Epic? The purpose of the story was to make him look good, god-like, stronger than ever. pg 101-102*

19. How do we know Gilgamesh was a famous king? *Gilgamesh was famous in the ancient world. Archaeology has unearthed tablets from Sumer, Babylon, Assyria, Canaan and the Hittite Empire with his name on them. pg 101*

20. If a man is known by his fruit, what might we conclude about Nimrod? *If a man is known by his fruit, what he produces, then The Rebel and Hunter of Men otherwise known as Nimrod must have been an evil man because Babylon was not a godly city. pg 103*

21. Is Gilgamesh Nimrod? *We may never know for sure if the Gilgamesh story was really about Nimrod. pg 102-103*

22. What is the most important thing to know about the *Epic of Gilgamesh? The important thing to remember about the Epic of Gilgamesh is it is not the real story of Noah. It is not the story that inspired the flood. The flood inspired it, and the Epic's purpose was to pervert the truth. pg 103*

23. Does the Bible say Nimrod built the Tower of Babel? *Some believe Nimrod was the man who led the people to build the Tower. The Bible does not say that. It says, "And they said," meaning the people. The word used for them is bên, son or children. pg 103-104*

24. What is the one ancient text we have that is whole and has guided archaeologists? *It is the Bible that is the only documentation which has endured into modern times whole. pg 104*

Activity: If we did not have the Bible as our guide, what might we think of the discoveries made by archaeologists? How would it change our view of history? If you never heard about a worldwide flood or a man named Noah, how would that change your understanding of the world? Ask someone else these same questions and write down what they say. Do you agree? *Answers will vary.*

25. What followed Nimrod's city building efforts? *Great empires followed. pg 104*

26. What does Dr. Johannes Krause's research tell us? *His studies have found Neanderthals had the same language gene as modern man. In other words he could speak. His other research has traced ancient Europeans to Mesopotamia. But in 2017 Dr. Krause discovered ancient Egyptians are also descended from people in the Near East. In fact, they have no sub-Saharan African genes, and are closely related to Europeans. The Near East is the Levant part of the Fertile Crescent. Krause's research doesn't support evolutional theory stating Egyptians migrated from the jungles of Africa. pg 105*

27. What is the most important thing to remember about evolutionists' theories about ancient man? *The important thing to know is evolutionists in archaeology are discovering their ideas for ancient man and what he knew and how he lived are wrong. He was smarter and more skilled than they thought. pg 106*

28. What are the problems with the evolutionists' timelines and charts for ancient man? *Problems with the chart include the ape/man, gatherer only, has never been found, and recent discoveries place intelligent builders, sculptors, pottery makers, metal workers, writers and farmers in the place of the missing ape/ archaic human. pg 106-107*

29. Briefly describe Noah's history before the flood and after. *Noah was also a farmer, before he became a ship builder and after. When Noah's family left the ark, God told them they could eat meat. All of them needed to eat. His children and grandchildren learned how to farm by helping him. They farmed, hunted, fished, gathered wild food, kept goats, sheep, cattle, birds and saved seeds to plant. The locations of the archaeologists' discoveries fit where Noah's children and grandchildren were first and where they traveled after their languages were changed. They began building cities, then empires. pg 107*

Activity: If all the evidence for the accuracy of the Bible were presented to someone, would it guarantee they would accept the Bible as true and worth investigating for themselves? Why or why not? Imagine you are talking to this person, what would you say? Write it down and go over it. Take turns practicing with a believing friend. You will be ready to share what you know when you get the chance. Never be afraid to speak the truth about God or be discouraged if the person doesn't listen to you. You spoke and God will take it from there. *Answers will vary.*

30. What is the major lesson Noah's life story teaches us? *The major lesson Noah teaches us is to take God's word seriously. When God told him about things he needed to prepare for, things no one had ever witnessed, he listened. Then he acted. He understood what God says happens. pg 111*

Chapter 7 Test Answers

1. Why do some say there was a pre-Adamite civilization? *Evolutionists face big challenges with the King List. They date the List to around 266,000 years ago. But they think apes became men around 200,000 years ago and they date the rise of civilization, including kings, to around 6,000 years ago. To solve the problem their dates create, they say there was a pre-Adamite civilization of archaic humans which became extinct. pg 94*

2. What does the Sumerian King List say about a flood? *After the listing of eight kings it says, "Then the flood swept over." pg 95*

3. What tower myth is connected to one of the kings on the List and what is the king's name? *Enmerkar is among the kings on the Sumerian King List. He is named as the second king of Uruk and its builder. Enmerkar and the Lord of Aratta tells the story of how Enmerkar wanted to build a temple for the god Enki at Eridu but was stopped because the languages were confused. He prayed for man to speak one language again. He said the god Enki had changed one language into many because of ambitious lords, princes and kings. pg 96*

4. Who is Gilgamesh and what is the name of his flood story? *Gilgamesh was the king of Uruk or Erech as the Bible spells it. (Iraq comes from the word Erech.) He is listed as the fifth king of Uruk on the Sumerian King List. His flood story is called The Epic of Gilgamesh. pg 97*

5. According to his story, what was Gilgamesh like? *Gilgamesh was handsome and strong. No one could beat him. He was lord over men according to the Epic, and he built the walls of Uruk with baked bricks and*

overlaid the exterior with copper. He went out into the lands around, and the Epic says "no son was left to his father" because he took them all. The women too. Before young girls could marry, they had to act like his wife. The people complained Gilgamesh was not a good king. He did not take care of the people like a shepherd would his sheep. pg 97

6. What are the similarities between Nimrod and Gilgamesh? *Both are described as powerful. Both are considered sinful and in opposition to the God who never sleeps and whose voice is like thunder. Nimrod lived during the time of Noah and witnessed younger generations born with shorter life spans. pg 100*

7. What truths are hidden in the *Epic of Gilgamesh*? *Gilgamesh, an early king wanted to know Utnapishtim's secret for long life. Utnapishtim is a Noah-like figure. Also, in Gilgamesh's story the serpent stole man's ability to live forever on the earth, a story Nimrod would have known about Adam and Eve. Some wonder if the god Huwawa is the YHWH (Yahweh) of the Bible. pf 100-101.*

8. What is the most important thing to know about the *Epic of Gilgamesh*? *The important thing to remember about the Epic of Gilgamesh is it is not the real story of Noah. It is not the story that inspired the flood. The flood inspired it, and the Epic's purpose was to pervert the truth. pg 103*

9. What does Dr. Johannes Krause's research tell us? *His studies have found Neanderthals had the same language gene as modern man. In other words he could speak. His other research has traced ancient Europeans to Mesopotamia. But in 2017 Dr. Krause discovered ancient Egyptians are also descended from people in the Near East. In fact, they have no sub-*

Saharan African genes, and are closely related to Europeans. The Near East is the Levant part of the Fertile Crescent. Krause's research doesn't support evolutional theory stating Egyptians migrated from the jungles of Africa. pg 105

10. What are the problems with the evolutionists' timelines and charts for ancient man? *Problems with the chart include the ape/man, gatherer only, has never been found, and recent discoveries place intelligent builders, sculptors, pottery makers, metal workers, writers and farmers in the place of the missing ape/ archaic human. pg 106-107*

Thank you for purchasing *NOAH* Study Guide. If you found it helpful, please leave a review online where you found the book. You can also contact us directly on our website at flyingeaglepublications.com. We would love to hear from you, and while you are there, sign up to receive emails alerting you to deals, offers and updates. Share us with your friends. Let's get the word out: the Bible is true and God is good!